# HOW TO PLAN & BUILD
# DECKS

**By the Editors of
Sunset Books and Sunset Magazine**

Lane Publishing Co. • Menlo Park, California

## We would like to thank . . .

. . . the many homeowners, architects, landscape architects, and designers whose talents have contributed to this new edition of *How to Build Decks*.

For their valuable consulting help, we particularly thank landscape architect Donald G. Boos, Robert A. Holcombe of the National Forest Products Association, Ian Martin of the California Redwood Association, and Raymond W. Moholt of Western Wood Products Association. We also are grateful to the following individuals who generously gave their help and advice: Tom Brogan of the Northern Hardwood and Pine Manufacturing Association; Barbara DiConza; Charles G. Gehring of the Southern Forest Products Association; Don Hatch, Ed McGeeney, and Ken Mosby of the Sunset Patio Shop; Robert W. Peterson; and Donald W. Vandervort.

## Supervising Editor: Barbara G. Gibson

Staff Editors:
Bob Thompson, Don Rutherford

Design:
Cynthia Hanson

Illustrations:
Rik Olson

Front cover:
Photographed by Steve W. Marley

Editor, Sunset Books: David E. Clark

Third Printing October 1981

# CONTENTS

## PLANNING YOUR DECK  4

First steps toward a functional deck: finding the right deck location, getting your plans on paper, working with professionals

## BUYER'S GUIDE TO BUILDING MATERIALS  15

A look at the options in construction materials for the three main parts of a deck: surface, substructure, and foundation

## DRAWING A WORKABLE DECK DESIGN  22

How to draw plans—for the deck surface, substructure, and foundation—that you or your builder can work from

## DECK IDEAS IN COLOR  32

To inspire your thinking, a sparkling collection of deck ideas that can make a yard more livable

## HOW TO ESTIMATE & ORDER MATERIALS  66

Cost-saving tips and techniques for estimating and ordering construction materials

## BUILDING YOUR DECK  70

The nuts and bolts of deck construction, from preparing the site to laying the decking

## PROTECTING YOUR INVESTMENT  84

What you should know about preservatives, finishes, and everyday maintenance

## LIVING WITH YOUR DECK  88

Ways to bring light, heat, and water into your new outdoor room

## CHARTS  93

Comparative guides to decking and other lumber, and to nails, screws, and bolts

## INDEX  96

### SPECIAL FEATURES

Deck Builder's Check List  14

Sample Materials List  67

The Building Sequence . . . from Start to Finish  72

Comparative Guide to Decking Lumber  95

# PLANNING YOUR DECK

**Good strategy is the key to every successful deck project. It means, in part:**

- **knowing your legal limits**
- **finding the best deck setting**
- **putting your plan on paper**
- **learning how an expert can help**

Sometimes the best room in the house is outside on the wood deck. Naturally versatile, a deck can be your breakfast room on sunny summer mornings, a play yard for youngsters, a sitting room for reading, a kitchen for cookouts, and a living room for garden parties. And, if you're a green thumb who's short on garden space, a deck can provide just the room you need to putter among your favorite container plants.

Happily, it's seldom necessary to have expert design and carpentry skills in order to design and build a simple wood deck. With proper planning, a few tools, and a little perseverance, a home carpenter can successfully convert yard space into deck space as long as the deck's design is fairly straightforward and uncomplicated. (Consider as a simple deck one measuring 8 by 10 feet, installed 1 foot above level ground and supported by concrete piers.)

Of course, the more complicated the deck design, the greater the skill required in planning and construction. That simple 8 by 10-foot deck becomes quite another project when it is raised 8 feet, rather than 1 foot, off the ground. Likewise, more sophisticated (if not professional) skills may be necessary for building the deck designed with built-in benches, railings, or steps, or for the deck that must be raised above unstable or sloping sites.

Whichever route you take toward a new deck—do it all, do some, or have it done—spend some time browsing through these pages on planning. They can help you understand legal codes and ordinances affecting home improvements, help you find the best location for your deck, and guide you in working with professionals when you want or need their expertise.

## Which deck is your best bet?

Decks fall into three categories: low-level, hillside, and roof decks.

*Low-level decks,* supported directly by concrete piers or on short posts, are often the simplest decks

*HIGH-LEVEL DECK*

*LOW-LEVEL DECK*

*ROOF DECK*

to build. Though generally more expensive on a cost-per-square-foot basis, low-level decks are often preferred to paved patios because wood is more resilient and reflects less heat than most masonry materials. Attached to the house or freestanding, low-level decks can be designed to suit a legion of different uses and settings. They make particularly effective solutions for damp or uneven locations.

*Hillside decks* offer the classic solution to a problem every hillside homeowner faces in making use of a steep lot—how to create level space where none exists. Though costlier than low-level decks or paved patios, and—depending on the situation—more difficult to build, hillside decks extend living space at a fraction of the cost required to add a full interior room.

*Roof decks* are often easy to install over a garage roof or a room designed to support deck loads. They can make wonderful private vantage points while they create outdoor living space. However, because they are frequently exposed to extremes in sun and wind, roof decks can present tricky challenges in landscaping and climate control.

Whichever deck suits your site and needs—low-level, hillside, or rooftop—the secret to making a success of your project lies in

1) planning, 2) planning, and 3) planning! Achieving a deck that accommodates a wide variety of family activities, suits your budget, and adds value to your property requires thoughtful attention to several separate factors.

• Size and shape limit the activities or uses of a deck.

• Location and access affect traffic inside the house for better or worse.

• At least four microclimates exist around the four sides of a house. Locating the deck in one or another of these shortens or lengthens its useful season.

• Solid knowledge of construction materials is vital to a sensible building budget, while equally solid knowledge of the legalities—building codes and zoning ordinances—is a major guarantee of property enhancement. With careless planning, on the other hand, you stand a high risk of having to live with a costly white elephant that suits neither your needs nor the style of your house—and may even depress the value of your house or make it harder to sell in the event you move.

## Know your legal limits

Early in your deck planning, pay a visit to your city or county building department to learn about the regulations which may affect the design and construction of your deck, and which (if any) building permits are required. Also, look over your property deed for limitations it may impose on your proposed addition.

Building codes and zoning laws may seem awesome in their breadth and meticulousness, but they are designed to protect you from faulty, possibly dangerous construction practices as well as property misuse. Bypassing them runs you the risk of having to bring your deck up to code with costly corrections, or dismantle it entirely if it violates zoning or building codes (or, perhaps, a right-of-way given a utility company in your deed). In addition, failure to get proper permits may result in a fine or other penalty.

### Typical code requirements

Building codes set minimum standards for home improvement design and construction, and for materials used in construction. They also occasionally place limits on the location of structures on the property.

In the case of decks, you can expect to find that codes call for certain materials in the foundation, specific spacing between joists in the substructure, and minimum weights the deck surface must be able to support. In addition, if you live in a fire-hazardous area, you may be required by local ordinances to use woods that have been chemically treated to resist fire.

### Typical building codes

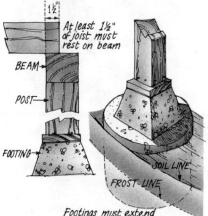

Footings must extend below frost line

If the deck you propose doesn't conform to the building code in your area, your city or county building department will specify what alterations are necessary to bring it up to code.

### Zoning laws

Zoning ordinances are designed primarily to regulate land use by establishing boundaries between residential, commercial, and industrial areas, but they also set limitations on land use within these boundaries. In residential zones, they limit the height of buildings, establish the maximum percentage of a lot the structure may cover, specify setback limitations (how close to the property line you can build), and, on occasion, control architectural design standards. (See illustration at right.)

**Variances.** It is possible to obtain a zoning variance if you can prove

(either to a hearing officer or zoning board of appeal) that the proposed deck will not encroach on a neighbor's privacy, and that precisely following zoning requirements would create "undue hardship." Applications for variances are available through your city or county planning department. A filing fee (ranging anywhere from $25 to $250) is usually required.

### Deed restrictions

Somewhere in your property deed may ride additional limitations that can affect the design, construction, or location of your deck. The deed may specify architectural design standards to which new structures must conform, or identify easements that give utility companies rights-of-way below and above ground, or—as in the case of condominiums—refer you to regulations established by a homeowners' association. Like building codes and zoning ordinances, deed restrictions have the effect of law. They can be changed only by mutual agreement among the parties, or by one party's winning a change in court.

### Building permits

Always get the necessary building permits before beginning construc-

tion. Simple deck projects may not require any permit, but complex ones usually call for separate permits for plumbing, wiring, carpentry work, and so on. Fees for permits are sometimes flat, sometimes based on the value of the improvement.

### Deciding your deck's location: the two-step inventory

Once you know the legal requirements on deck design and construction, the time has come for a two-step inventory to help decide the deck's location. First, consider your needs, then evaluate the potentials of your property. Although the deck's setting will be dictated largely by the size of your property and how your house sits on it, considering alternative sites will help you make the most of your opportunities.

### How will you use the deck?

With an eye toward the way you live, decide what functions you want the deck to serve. If you enjoy entertaining, you may want to situate it within easy reach of the kitchen, living room, or dining room. If you want a

**Zoning laws & deed restrictions: What they regulate**

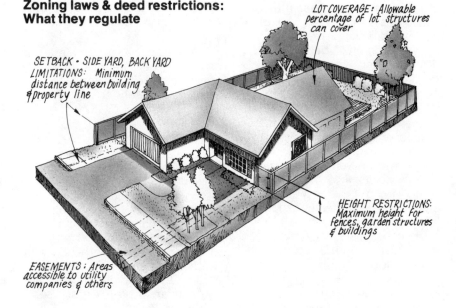

private spot for sunning or reading, you may want to open up a bedroom wall, put the deck right outside, and surround it with a privacy screen. If your deck will be the only place small children have to play, you may want to locate it where you can maintain a watchful eye. Perhaps your favorite pastime is gardening; a freestanding deck away from the house may give you a perfect garden sitting spot.

## Look over the landscape

Next, take stock of your property and evaluate its physical assets and liabilities—even if you plan to engage the services of a landscape architect or architect. Having a good understanding of your existing landscape will help you set priorities for a deck site, especially if you can situate the deck to take advantage of a pleasant view, or the shade of a mature garden tree, or a welcome southern exposure.

Landscape handicaps—perhaps a perilously steep lot, unstable soil conditions, too much yard exposed to busy street traffic, or too much shade (or sun, or wind)—also will affect the deck's location or call for design features that minimize these special problems (see page 11, "Decks that need a professional hand").

## Understanding your climates

Since the warmth or coolness of your deck will be decided largely by its orientation, it is wise to study the microclimates of your property along with the regional climate. Seasonal paths of the sun and prevailing winds can be affected greatly by a building, trees, or other obstructions on or near your property.

A deck in almost any location may serve well in midsummer, but wise planning can extend the outdoor season by several months.

### The general outlook

If you've lived in your present area a number of years, you should have a feeling for the general climate in terms of average seasonal air temperatures, rain and/or snowfall patterns, prevailing wind directions, and number of sunny days.

If not, you can get accurate climate information for your area from a number of agencies. One useful source of climate information is the National Oceanic and Atmospheric Administration (NOAA, pronounced "Noah"), National Climatic Center, Asheville, NC 28801. Send 20 cents with a request for the current annual issue of the Local Climatological Data for your area. You also may be able to get accurate climate information through U.S. Weather Bureau offices, public power and utility companies, meteorology departments on college and university campuses, and agricultural extension offices.

No matter how much official information you are able to gather, take personal stock of local weather as well as you can. Your neighborhood almost certainly will vary somewhat from the recording stations.

### Your relation to the sun

A deck's exposure to sun is one of the most important factors in climate control. Understanding the sun's path over your property may prompt you to extend the dimensions of your proposed deck or adjust its design in order to add a few weeks or months of sun or shade to your outdoor room.

Theoretically the deck that faces north is cooler because the sun rarely shines on it. A south-facing deck is usually warm because, from sunrise to sunset, the sun never leaves it. Decks on the east side stay cool, receiving only morning sun; and west-facing decks can be uncomfortably hot because they absorb the full force of the sun's midafternoon rays.

But beware of this oversimplified "hot western, warm southern, cool eastern, and cold northern" system. If you live in Phoenix, Arizona, for instance, where summer temperatures often climb above 100°F/38°C, a north-facing deck could hardly be considered cold. Likewise, a south-facing deck in San Francisco seldom can be thought of as warm, or a west-facing deck hot, because stiff ocean breezes and chilly fogs are frequent summertime visitors. Your regional climate may not be as exaggerated as these examples, but it will be definite enough to help you decide which exposure best lends itself to your requirements.

**Seasonal sunshine.** Another consideration is the sun's seasonal influence. As the sun crosses the sky, it makes an arc that changes slightly every day, becoming higher in the summer, lower in the winter. Long days in summer and short ones in winter alter sun and shade patterns on your deck, as shown in the illustrations below.

*9 hours of daylight*    WINTER

*12 hours of daylight*    FALL & SPRING

*15 hours of daylight*    SUMMER

## Neither wind, nor rain, nor snow...

...should be permitted to threaten your enjoyment of the deck you so painstakingly designed and built. Unfortunately, the elements can do more than chase you indoors if not taken into full account. Winds have been known to lift improperly anchored hillside decks off their substructures, snow sliding off rooftops has snapped many a fragile railing, and heavy rains have dislodged deck foundations on sites with poor drainage.

**Understanding wind.** Too much wind blowing over your deck on a cool day can be just as unpleasant as no breeze at all on a hot summer day. If you understand wind patterns around your house, you'll be better able to control or encourage them with fences, screens, or plants.

One balmy spring day, noting that the outside thermometer reads 68°F/20°C, you go outside for some sunning and reading. After an hour or so of toasty comfort, you suddenly feel cold, as if the temperature was nearer 60°F than 70. The thermometer still reads 68°F but a breeze has sprung up, and you're experiencing wind chill, one of the cooling effects of wind. We experience another cooling effect of wind when our bodies are wet, when we emerge from a pool, for example. That's evaporative cooling. Because of differences in weight, skin area, and metabolic rates, the loss of body heat caused by the wind varies between individuals.

Three different kinds of winds may influence your deck's location or design: annual prevailing winds, very localized seasonal breezes (daily, late afternoon, or summer), and occasional high-velocity winds generated by stormy weather. Even if the deck you propose faces only occasional strong winds, you may have to strengthen its foundation and substructure. Or if it faces only mild prevailing breezes, you may wish to modify them with a vertical screen that may or may not require structural attachment to the framing.

Before you design a vertical screen to diffuse wind, look at the following wind control study; it shows that solid barriers aren't necessarily the best ones. In the illustrations below, figures indicate the number of feet from the fence.

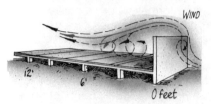

**Wind washes over a solid fence** as a stream of water would wash over a solid barrier. About the distance equal to fence height, protection drops rapidly.

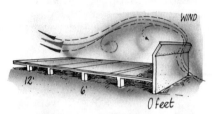

**Angling baffle into the wind** gives greatest protection close to the fence, but effective protection also extends to a distance more than twice fence height.

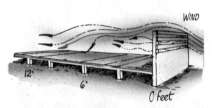

**Wind flow is broken** with a fence of wood strips spaced 1 to 2 inches apart. Up close, the fence offers somewhat less protection; temperatures are warmest 6 to 12 feet away. Screens of plants or dense shrubbery would yield more shelter.

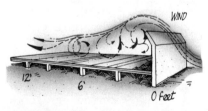

**A 45° baffle at top of fence** eliminates downward crash of wind. You feel warmest in the pocket below the baffle and up to 8 feet from the 6-foot-high fence.

**Regard the rain.** If in assessing your climate you learn that storms generally blow out of the northeast, you may wish to locate your deck where it won't take such a beating from the weather—perhaps on the south side of the house where it can be partly protected by trees or a roof overhang.

If you live in an area frequented by brief summer cloudbursts, you can extend the deck's usefulness with a roof that lets you sit outdoors during warm-weather rains. Like wind-screens, deck roofs often call for advance planning so they can be linked to the deck substructure (see page 28).

**Dealing with snow.** In areas of snowfall, decks are most frequently damaged by the weight of snow gathering in drifts or avalanching off gabled roofs. Snow is deceptively heavy; piled 5 to 6 feet deep on a deck, snow can weigh as much as 80 to 100 pounds per square foot—twice the maximum deck load allowed by municipal ordinances in many mild-climate regions. In areas of extremely heavy snowfall, the standing weight of snow alone can snap railings, crush benches, and collapse substructures of improperly designed decks.

Plan to strengthen the parts of your deck likely to take snow-load abuse. As much as possible, design the deck so railings are a safe distance from rooftop avalanches. The upright members of railings always should be securely bolted to the deck's substructure.

## The rehearsal: putting your plans on paper

Experimenting with your ideas on paper is one of the most practical ways to visualize your deck in different settings, and to try out design ideas you may have collected from home remodeling magazines and books. You don't have to be an artist to test your ideas with a pencil; the purpose of paper planning is simply to rough out as many ideas as possible with simple scale drawings.

A scale drawing should consist

of a base map on graph paper and overlay sheets of tracing paper. The base map shows house and lot. The tracing paper allows you to sketch ideas for decks one after another without redrawing the base each time. These drawings will show you how well each deck idea is "working": how well it meets your priorities, how well it encourages logical traffic patterns, how well it suits the house-garden relationship, and whether or not its size balances interior rooms of the house.

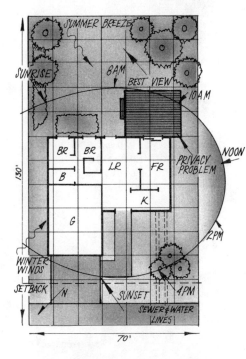

You'll save hours of complicated measuring if you can obtain copies of a surveyor's plot plan, architect's drawings or house plans, or contour maps that illustrate vital statistics of lot and buildings.

*Plot plans* (surveyor's drawings) usually locate your property and show streets, property corners, and distances between corners, plus the locations of any structures on the site when the lot was surveyed. Available through your county recorder or title company, these plans make an excellent starting point for your base map; simply transfer information from the plot plan to your graph paper.

*Architect's drawings* usually show site plan, floor plan, elevations, and foundation details. *Contour maps* show the shape of your site in 1-foot, 5-foot, and 10-foot contours—especially helpful if you are designing a deck for a hillside lot. Look for contour maps from your county engineer or department of public works.

## How to make a scale drawing

To make a scale drawing, you'll need graph paper (preferably four squares to the inch), a pad of tracing paper, and plenty of sharpened pencils (and erasers).

**The base map.** Use the largest scale the graph paper will allow, usually ¼ inch per linear foot. Show the following:

• Dimensions of your lot.
• Location of your house on lot, as well as doors and windows and the rooms from which they open.
• Points of the compass—north, south, east, and west.
• Path of the sun and any possible hot spots it creates.
• Direction of prevailing winds and winter storms.
• Existing plants and trees.
• Utilities (such as gas, and sewers or septic tanks) and depth of each (your utility companies can help you pin down this information), underground wires, exterior outlets for water and electricity; meter boxes and air conditioning units you may want to screen.
• Locations of easements or other rights-of-way contained in the deed to your property.
• Any problems beyond the lot line which may affect sun, view, or privacy, such as unsightly telephone wires, major plantings, a neighbor's second-story window, or traffic noise.

**Finding north.** If you don't already have a plan of your property showing its relationship to north, you can find magnetic north quite easily with an inexpensive magnetic compass, right angle square, and the completed base map of your house and lot. (Since true north and magnetic north are not always in agreement, you may wish to check a topographic map in your library or talk to a surveyor to learn how to correct for your area.)

First, find a flooring crack or carpet seam that parallels a main wall and align the scale wall in your drawing with the seam or crack (see illustration below):

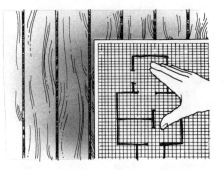

Next, lay a compass on the graph paper, locate north, and draw a line representing north. Add directions for east, south, and west with a right angle square.

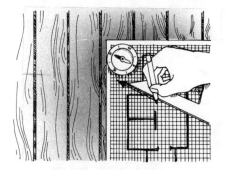

## Planning pointers from the drawing board

Once your base map is completed, lay a sheet of tracing paper over it and begin trying out your ideas. Keeping your priorities in mind, sketch as many deck designs as you can come up with, replacing the tracing paper with each new plan. As you experiment:

• *Try to see your design as a whole.* Your deck is both part of the garden and part of the house, so its size, design, and location will have an effect on both. If, for instance, you put the deck next to the living room, how will it affect the interior view of the garden? Will it eliminate valuable garden or play space? Will it allow adequate access from one to the other? Will its design reflect the house/garden atmosphere?

• *Plan generously—and then count costs.* Creating a strong design will help you distinguish between the more and less important elements of your plan so that you know where to make compromises to bring it within your budget. You may decide, for example, that you'd rather have a few extra feet in deck surface than a storage center, or built-in benches rather than the extra floor space.

• *Rely on familiar shapes.* Landscape designs based on squares, rectangles, hexagons, and circles almost always generate eye-pleasing designs (and are usually most economical to build). Avoid squiggly or arbitrarily curved patterns.

• *Think in three dimensions.* This will help you to balance the design elements and visualize the results. It will also keep you from confining your design to an endless horizontal plane.

• *Maintain a sense of proportion.* Your deck should be large enough to suit your varying needs, and large enough to accommodate outdoor furniture comfortably, but not so large that it overwhelms the landscape, your house, or you. Likewise, a deck that is dwarfed by house and garden can seem overcrowded with even the barest furnishings. As a general rule of thumb, try to size your deck so it complements, not dominates, the interior room or rooms from which it projects. A deck that wraps around the house, for example, may be generously sized where it joins the living room, a little smaller where it opens off the kitchen, and intimately small where it extends the master bath.

• *Look for a feeling of unity.* Elements in deck design—the shape, the pattern of the deck floor, railings, built-in benches, vertical screens, and roofs—should look as if they belong together. And, as a whole, the deck should blend with the architectural style of the house. If the house is built of rustic materials, the deck should be built of rustic materials; if the house has an uncluttered, formal feeling to it, the deck's design and appearance should reflect the same feeling.

• *Consider traffic patterns.* Traffic should move smoothly from house to deck and deck to garden. If you have to open up a wall to facilitate better circulation, avoid producing traffic patterns that run through the middle of rooms (see illustrations below).

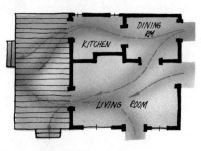

**Awkward** traffic pattern flows through centers of rooms.

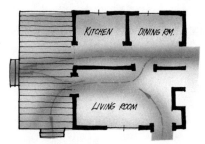

**Improved** traffic pattern flows along room perimeters.

• *Learn to stretch a low-level deck.* If you are planning a low-level deck, you can make it seem larger if you plan it around one or two planting areas. A simple 10 by 18-foot deck (see sketch below) can

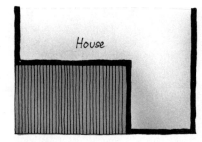

appear twice as large if you add 10 square feet of decking and two planting areas:

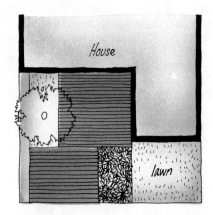

You can also make the space seem larger by linking the deck to the lawn and a single planting unit.

Or try connecting the deck to a paved area; you will expand living space without having to add to the deck surface or losing the warm feeling of the wood.

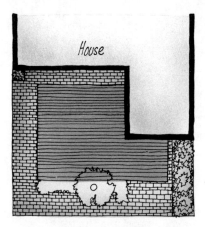

• *Look below a high-level deck.* If you're planning a high-level deck, consider what happens to the space beneath it. The deck will affect the temperature, view, light, and noise level of the area it overhangs (see illustration on next page).

A high-level deck will affect temperature when it casts a shadow on one of the house walls and cools related interior rooms, sometimes the year around. It affects the view when, looking through a lower-level window, all you see is the deck's

## Looking below a high-level deck

Noise from deck activities can carry into interior rooms below

Deck shadows can cool & darken lower level rooms

The view from below takes in the decks substructure

Plants may not thrive in the deep shade of the deck

underpinnings and an absence of landscaping because of a steep slope, fire hazard, or lack of light. In addition, high-level decks can block out daylight and transmit noises generated by deck activities into the rooms below.

You can minimize these handicaps by situating the deck above a windowless wall of the house, building a second deck at the lower level (costly), or designing the deck with a streamlined substructure (difficult).

## The last lap: should you do it yourself or work with professionals?

How much of the final deck design and/or construction you do yourself should depend on the time, energy, skill, and experience you can give the project, and on the extent of the work involved.

Building a basic wood deck up to 8 feet above fairly level ground should offer no serious problems to the home carpenter with a few free weekends or evenings. Certain terrain conditions and some types of decks, though, call for partial or complete professional handling.

## When you do the work yourself

When you decide to do all of the work yourself, you become your own jack-of-all-trades, changing hats as you become architect, contractor, plumber, carpenter, electrician—whatever is required to get the job done.

The obvious reason for deciding to design and build your own deck (aside from the sheer satisfaction

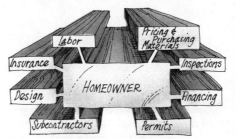

you get seeing your own handiwork) is keeping the cost of the project down. Bypassing professional landscape architects, architects, and contractors eliminates professional fees and material markups from your costs. Though not all-inclusive, the "Deck builder's check list" (page 14) is designed to serve as your informal guide through the home remodeler's labyrinth.

## Decks that need a professional hand

You should consult with a professional if you plan to build a high-level or cantilevered deck or a deck on an unstable site, or if you are going to use materials such as concrete or tile—they may require structural consideration.

**Sites over sand, mud, or water.** Lakeside and beach locations often require special pilings for the deck support structure. The design and placement of piling substructures are jobs for specialists, although once pilings and beams are in place, remaining construction should present no special problems.

**Unstable soil.** If your lot is steep, check out its soil stability with your building department before you begin construction. Deck foundations which are installed on slopes subject to earth slides must usually be designed by, or have the approval of, a professional structural or soils engineer.

**Leakproof deck surfaces.** Roofing contractors are good sources of information for homeowners planning to build a roof deck that requires a waterproof surface in order to keep rooms below the deck dry. Concrete, tile, fiberglass, and liquid rubber coatings all can be used successfully to create a watertight surface, though the extra weight of some require additional structural support.

**High-level decks.** Generally speaking, the higher the deck, the harder it is to build. The do-it-yourself remodeler working at more than an arm's reach overhead will find it difficult getting posts in plumb (true vertical), placing and leveling beams, and squaring the deck's framework. Decks at extreme heights also often require special design techniques . . . a job for professionals. If yours is a high-level deck, you can contract construction of the framework and then complete the work tailored to your abilities.

**Cantilevering.** Like many balconies, cantilevered decks are sup-

**Decks that need a professional hand**

CANTILEVERED DECKS

LOAD-BEARING DECKS

DECKS WITH WEATHERTIGHT SURFACES

DECKS OVER WATER

ported by joists or beams which extend into and are anchored by the house structure. In this way they are self-supporting; attempting to add a self-supporting deck to a house is usually impractical because of the specialized skills required. (Nearly all cantilevered decks are built with the house.) A freestanding deck might have one end securely anchored to a concrete foundation in the hillside, the other end cantilevered over posts (see cantilevered deck above). Design and construction are best left to professionals.

**Opening up a wall.** The job of opening up a wall to create easier access from house to deck is, though not out of reach of the amateur carpenter, an exacting

one. An exterior wall that serves as a bearing wall (it holds up the roof or floor above) must be able to support the same load when altered. In addition, you may uncover plumbing pipes and fixtures or wiring that must be relocated. If you're unsure whether or not this job is one you can handle, consult with a professional. (To learn more about opening up a wall, see the *Sunset* book *Basic Carpentry Illustrated.*)

## Which professional—& when?

By training and experience, landscape architects, architects, landscape and building designers, structural and soils engineers,

building and landscape contractors, drafters, and subcontractors all can, to one degree or another, provide you with professional design and/or construction assistance.

**Landscape architects and architects.** Many homeowners retain the services of professional architects or landscape architects when they consider home improvements. Architects and landscape architects are state-licensed professionals with bachelor's or master's degrees in architecture or landscape architecture, and they are trained to create designs that are structurally sound, functional, and esthetically pleasing. They also know the ins and outs of construction materials, understand the mechanics of estimating, can negotiate bids from contractors, and can supervise the actual work.

At least three options are open to you if you choose to include in your project either an architect or landscape architect.

Retained on a consultation basis, an architect or landscape architect will review your scale drawings, perhaps suggest ideas for a more effective design, perhaps provide a couple of rough conceptual sketches. Fees for simple consultations usually range from $20 to $50 (sometimes more) per hour.

You also may hire a professional to design your deck and provide working drawings; you then become responsible for the construction. For the design and working drawings you may be charged either a flat or hourly fee.

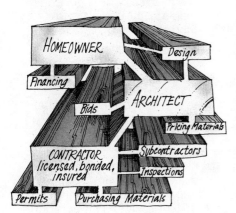

Third, you can retain a landscape architect or architect on a planning-through-construction basis. Besides designing your deck and providing working drawings and specifications, he or she will draw up bid forms, negotiate bids, arrange contracts with general contractors or subcontractors, see that correct grades of construction materials are used as specified, and supervise construction. It will cost you more (usually 10 to 15 percent of the cost of the work) to have your deck designed and built this way, but you will also be free from the plethora of details you otherwise would have to handle.

**Landscape and building designers.** A landscape designer usually has a landscape architect's education and training but does not have a landscape architect's state license. With a contractor's license, a designer can help you design your deck, but by law he or she may also have to do the installation.

Building designers, licensed (by the American Institute of Building Designers) or unlicensed, also may offer design services in conjuction with project construction.

**Structural and soils engineers.** If you are planning a deck over an unstable or steep lot, your building department may require that you (or your landscape architect) consult with a soils or structural engineer before your plans are approved.

Soils engineers evaluate soil conditions on a proposed construction site and establish design specifications for foundations that can resist whatever stresses unstable soil exerts.

Structural engineers, often working with the calculations a soils engineer provides, design foundation piers and footings to suit the site. In the case of decks, they also may provide wind and load stress calculations as the building department requires.

**General and landscape contractors.** Licensed general and landscape contractors specialize in construction (landscape contractors specialize in garden construction), though some also have design skills and experience as well. Their fees for designing usually are lower than a landscape architect's, but their design skills may be limited by a construction point of view.

Contractors called on to build a small project may do the work them-

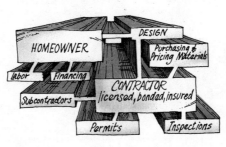

selves. On a large project they assume the responsibility for hiring qualified subcontractors, ordering construction materials, and seeing that the job is completed according to contract (see page 14).

**Subcontractors.** If you act as your own general contractor, it's up to you to hire and supervise whatever subcontractors (specialists in carpentry, grading, plumbing, electrical work, and the like) the job requires. You're not limited to working with subcontractors. You can hire workers with the necessary skills, but you will be responsible for insurance and payroll taxes as well as direct supervision.

Aside from doing work according to the working drawings you provide, subcontractors can often supply you with current product information and sell hardware and supplies.

When dealing with subcontractors, give them clear instructions, put all firm agreements in writing, and provide as much direct supervision as you can. Don't try to supervise a subcontractor's employees, though.

Trade associations can recommend licensed subcontractors in your area; check the Yellow Pages under "Associations" or "Labor Organizations" for the phone number of the local branch. Recommendations from other homeowners will also help you locate reliable and competent subcontractors.

**Drafters.** Drafters may be unlicensed apprentices to architects or they may be members of a skilled trade. They can make the working drawings which are required before you can secure building permits, drawings from which you or your contractor can work. They also may design structures with wood-frame construction.

## Choosing a professional

The best way to choose a landscape architect, architect, designer, or contractor is to see the person's work. If you don't already have someone in mind, check the Yellow Pages under "Landscape Architects," "Architects," "Landscape Contractors," "Landscape Designers," or "Building Designers."

Though some excellent professional designers have no professional affiliation, many belong to the American Society of Landscape Architects (ASLA), American Institute of Architects (AIA), American Institute of Building Designers (AIBD), or a state landscape contractors' association. To locate members in your area, contact a nearby office.

Finding a reliable contractor may take some time if you haven't retained a landscape architect or architect who can recommend qualified people. The larger general contractors usually have projects scheduled months in advance and rarely take on small jobs.

Talk with homeowners who have had or are having work done, or material suppliers or subcontractors who depend on contractors' business.

When selecting a contractor, base your decision on the individual's reputation in home building rather than on the lowest bid. The contractor you choose should be well established, cooperative, competent, financially solvent (check bank and credit references), and insured for worker's compensation, property damage, and public liability.

Then try to get estimates from several contractors whose work you have found to be reliable. At this stage you are under no obligation to hire a contractor, and the contractor is likewise under no obligation to make a commitment to you.

## The contract

A solid contract should include detailed drawings, descriptions of all construction materials, descriptions of all work to be performed, a time schedule for the project, and method of payment.

**Construction materials.** The contract should identify all construction materials by brand name, quality markings (especially with lumber species and grades), and model numbers where applicable.

**Work to be performed.** Work you expect the contractor to do should be clearly stated in the contract. If, for example, you want the contractor to prepare the site, the contract should explicitly identify appropriate tasks: remove fences and shrubs, tear out concrete, grade, and so forth.

**Time schedule.** Though a contractor cannot be responsible for construction delays caused by strikes and material shortages, he or she should assume responsibility for a reasonable time limit for project completion. Your best leverage is a stipulation that the final payment will be withheld until work is finished.

**Method of payment.** The contract should also specify how payments are to be made. This is usually done in either of two ways: one payment at the beginning and the other on completion of the project, or in installments as work progresses.

---

## Deck Builder's Check List

### First Steps

1. Decide deck functions (page 6)    ✓
2. Evaluate your microclimate (page 7) _____
3. Check property title for deed restrictions and easements (page 5) _____
4. Visit building department, planning department for building codes and zoning ordinances (pages 5–6) _____
5. Obtain site plan, architect's drawings, and contour maps (page 9) _____

### Designing The Deck

1. Draw base map (page 9) _____
2. Make preliminary sketches of deck _____
3. Take sketches to landscape architect, architect, or designer (optional) _____
4. Take sketches to building department _____
5. Get ballpark estimate on materials, construction (pages 66–69) _____
6. Prepare (or have drafter prepare) working drawings of deck (pages 13, 22–31) _____

### Permits, Materials & Contracts

1. Get permits from building department _____
2. Prepare materials list (page 69) _____
3. Price materials at different suppliers _____
4. Select contractor (optional); draw up contract (page 14) _____
5. Arrange financing _____
6. Arrange for worker's compensation and other insurance, withholding tax and Social Security contributions if necessary _____

### Construction

1. Purchase materials and begin construction (pages 66–93) _____
2. Arrange for building inspector to check various stages of work at appropriate times _____

---

# BUYER'S GUIDE TO BUILDING MATERIALS

**Will your deck
do what you want it to do?
Look the way you want it to look?
If you choose the right materials,
it will.**

One major step you'll take in designing your deck is choosing materials for its three main parts: surface, substructure, and foundation (see sketch below).

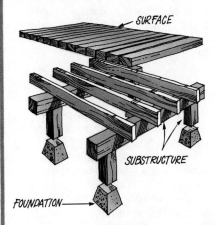

Surfaces usually are wood, but they can be tile, concrete, or a synthetic material over wood subflooring. The synthetics include fiberglass, outdoor carpeting, and a number of nonskid coatings, some of which are applied like paint.

Wood is the favorite choice for elements of the substructure, too—posts, beams, and, where design calls for them, joists. Steel is sometimes used for any or all of these parts; concrete may be used for posts.

Foundations are almost invariably built of concrete, though occasionally decks may have foundations of treated posts or pilings set directly in the earth.

Start with the topside when you make your material choices. Decks are built from the ground up but planned from the top down, because the nature and weight of the deck surface governs the type and design of the substructure and foundation.

As you compare materials, weigh their cost against appearance, durability, and suitability to your construction needs.

## Deck surface materials: Your options

Weight is the key consideration when you choose deck flooring;

the greater the deck's weight, the stronger the substructure must be. Other factors may outrank weight as a consideration, though. Where a weathertight deck is required, concrete may be the best choice in spite of its great weight. Appearance, durability, and cost are other factors to consider in choosing a deck surface.

## Wood surfaces

Wood is the favorite in deck surfacing materials—and with good reason: wood is resilient underfoot, low in heat reflection, and durable (true of even the less-hardy species that have been properly treated with preservatives). Compared to other decking materials, it is easily handled by the do-it-yourself enthusiast because it can be worked with common tools and weighs about 4 pounds per square foot for 2-inch lumber.

You can choose from a variety of species and grades (see "Buyer's guide to decking lumber," pages 20–21) to meet particular budget, structural and appearance requirements. You also can create almost any floor pattern using 2 by 2s, 2 by 4s, or 2 by 6s (see page 23), though the more complicated patterns are usually more costly to build. For wood finishes you can decide among stains, paints, bleaches, or sealers—or you can use nothing at all if you want the deck to weather naturally (see pages 84–87, "Protecting your investment").

Wood, of course, does have its disadvantages: it is vulnerable to fires; in most species it is susceptible to decay and termites; and it requires periodic maintenance. One drawback important to those who plan a room below the deck is that wood must generally be used in conjunction with other materials to provide a weathertight surface.

**Decking lumber.** Standard dimension lumber is most commonly used for decking. This category includes 2 by 2s, 2 by 3s, 2 by 4s, and 2 by 6s, all spaced slightly apart to allow for adequate drainage and expansion and contraction of the wood. Because 2 by 8s and wider

tend to "cup" (warp crosswise), they seldom are used.

Tongue-and-groove (T&G) lumber, milled so its edges interlock (see illustration below), is used for sheltered decks having a solid wood surface. T&G planks are normally

SQUARE EDGE     TONGUE & GROOVE (T&G)

2 inches thick and 6 or 8 inches wide. Special care must be taken when tongue-and-groove lumber is used for decking, however, because fitted boards tend to swell and buckle in moist weather, shrink and separate in dry weather. Boards must be laid to accommodate these changes without separating. They must also be well treated with a waterproof finish so moisture cannot collect in the joints.

Board lumber, 1 inch or thinner, can be used as decking. It costs less than 2-inch dimension lumber but requires many more joists for support, making it uneconomical in some cases.

**Wood subflooring.** Wood subfloors, built with either T&G boards or exterior plywood, often serve as a base for decks surfaced with concrete, tile, fiberglass, or rubberized coatings.

T&G lumber considered suitable for subflooring measures either 1 by 4 or 1 by 6. It is usually the less expensive "Common" grade.

Exterior plywood, available in 4 by 8-foot panels, provides a stronger subfloor than T&G boards, is economical, and easy to lay. Be sure to order *exterior* plywood for decks. Interior plywood types (including the kind made with exterior glues) must not be used outdoors.

Standard thicknesses range from ¼ to 1¼ inches in ⅛-inch increments; those ¾ inch and greater (⅞, 1, 1⅛, and 1¼ inch) are recommended for subflooring.

For interlocking panels, 4 by 8-foot sheets come with both narrow

and long edges cut in tongue-and-groove fashion. With this type, blocked-in backing between joists is not required beneath the panels' edges.

## Concrete, tile & fiberglass

If your goal is to build a solid-surfaced deck, perhaps one that is weathertight, you can choose from a number of other deck materials, including concrete, tile, fiberglass, or nonskid coatings. Most can be installed over an inexpensive wood subfloor built of 1 by 4 or 1 by 6 tongue-and-groove boards or ¾-inch or thicker plywood. Instructions for installing each type of material are available from suppliers and manufacturers.

**Concrete surfaces.** A concrete surface offers the advantages of relatively low material costs, high durability, fire resistance, freedom from decay, and watertightness. But a concrete deck is not a project for the do-it-yourself builder. The weight of freshly poured concrete is formidable; even when dry and cured, a single square foot of lightweight concrete, 3 inches thick, weighs almost 30 pounds. The job requires special skills and equipment, special reinforced deck design, and hard physical work. Consult an architect, engineer, or contractor if you want a concrete deck.

**Tile surfaces.** Successfully laying a tile deck surface is well within the capabilities of most home builders, provided the work is done carefully. Professional advice on deck design is recommended.

Tile decking is comparable in weight to concrete roof and decking mixes. Placed on a 1-inch mortar base, tile weighs about 20 pounds per square foot and requires much stronger support systems and foundations than a wooden deck.

The chief disadvantage of tile is its relatively high cost. Depending on the type, tile ranks among the most expensive of deck surfacing materials. For detailed information on tile decking, see the *Sunset* book

*How to Build Walks, Walls & Patio Floors.*

**Fiberglass.** "Glassing" is one way to obtain a watertight deck surface. Comparable in overall cost to all-wood decking, fiberglass installation consists of laying a special mat (called "roving") onto the subflooring and then applying coats of polyester resin. The clear resin is often pigmented for color and dusted with 30-mesh aggregate sand for traction. The work is generally considered a do-it-yourself project, but beware: follow manufacturer's instructions carefully.

A fiberglass deck is durable, termiteproof, and rot-free (though its subflooring is not). Its main disadvantages are that it strongly reflects heat and light and that it needs recoating with resin or paint every 4 or 5 years. For modern decks, fiberglass replaces the time-honored waterproofing materials of canvas and "boot-topping" paint.

**Nonskid surfaces.** Various kinds of nonskid materials are used on deck surfaces that are likely to become slippery—around swimming pools, on ramps, and so forth. Some of these materials are painted or spread on decks; others come in sheets or rolls that are glued in place with adhesives. Sources for information on these materials include swimming pool suppliers, marine equipment firms, and, in some areas, paint and hardware stores or lumberyards.

**Outdoor carpeting.** Woven of synthetics, exterior carpeting is highly durable and resistant to fading, soil, stain, rot, mildew, fire, and insects. As a deck covering, it offers good traction, deadens sound, and remains cool underfoot on hot days.

A major disadvantage of outdoor carpeting is that it requires more general upkeep than other deck surfacings. Leaves and conifer needles are difficult to sweep off. Stains are often more conspicuous, demanding prompt treatment, and periodic cleaning with a wet or dry rug shampoo is advisable. Outdoor carpeting is also relatively expensive. And

since carpeting doesn't add to the strength of a deck, subflooring must provide the necessary support.

## The substructure: Joists, beams & posts

The supporting framework below a deck's surface (moving from the top down) consists of joists, beams, posts or their equivalents, and, when required, cross bracing. Materials used for these members include lumber, concrete, steel posts, and steel structurals (aluminum beams are used in some cases). The selection of materials usually depends on their inherent strength for the particular deck situation.

Sometimes appearance and economy must be sacrificed for proper strength. Any wood that is nearer than 6 inches to the ground or concrete should be a durable species or pressure-treated to resist decay. Use either foundation-grade redwood, cedar, or wood that has been pressure-treated with preservative.

### Dimension lumber

Simple to work with and readily available, dimension lumber is the most commonly used substructure material. Typical dimension lumber comes in 2 and 4-inch thicknesses in widths of 2, 4, 6, 8, 10, and 12 inches.

If you need larger dimensions than are available, you can sometimes nail or bolt two or more pieces together to form the larger dimensions. For example, you can form a 6 by 10-inch beam by sandwiching three 2 by 10s (though the 2 by 10s, which together measure 4½ inches, will not be as strong as a single 6 by 10, whose finished thickness is 5½ inches). Likewise, you can add to the maximum standard length of lumber (24 feet) by sandwiching and offset splicing (see page 74). Or you can splice shorter pieces together to the lengths you need if you want to make the most efficient use of the lumber you buy.

### Poles, piling & timbers

Certain features of the terrain or home sometimes require the use of single-piece wood posts or beams larger than those that are generally available. Substitutes can range in sophistication from home-cut trees to high-cost, custom-laminated beams.

**Poles.** Natural poles make particularly good posts for decks of rustic cabins and beach houses. They may be treated with preservatives, untreated, or used with the tree bark attached.

Pole diameters should be governed by the scale of the house and the weight they must support. A small house can be dwarfed by massive logs; a large house can make small-diameter poles look spindly. Building codes determine how much weight each size pole can bear, and whether they should be pressure-treated with preservatives.

**Piling.** Wood used for posts of decks over sand, mud, and water should be in the form of piling—a system of large-diameter, specially treated poles. For large decks, steel piling (pipe or beam-shaped) may be used instead. Though piling should be installed by professional specialists, once it's in place it lends itself to do-it-yourself completion of the deck.

**Timbers.** All milled lumber with both width and thickness 5 inches and greater is classified "timber." Timbers are commonly used for beams spanning longer distances and for posts subject to severe loads.

A variation of single-piece timbers are laminated wood structural beams, custom manufactured in straight, arched, or curved shapes to span 30 feet or more. They are expensive and are limited in use to professionally designed decks.

### Concrete columns

Increasingly popular as deck posts are cylindrical concrete columns. Temporary fiber tube forms are set in place and filled with concrete, forming maintenance-free columns that offer complete protection

**Typical substructure materials**

DIMENSION LUMBER

CONCRETE COLUMNS

STEEL POSTS

NATURAL POLES

against fire, termites, and decay.

Available in some building supply stores, fiber tube forms come in standard 6 to 24-inch diameters. Their cost depends upon their diameter. They can be cut to size with a carpenter's saw.

Another kind of form popularly used for pouring concrete columns is ordinary clay sewer pipe. Standard pipe sizes include 1, 2, 3, and 5-foot lengths; diameters are 4, 6, and 8 inches. Unlike fiber tube forms, clay pipe forms are left permanently in place.

The handling of concrete requires hard physical labor. For the do-it-yourself builder, this type of column should be limited to heights less than 3 feet above foundations. Pouring columns of greater heights requires special experience in concrete reinforcing,

mixing, and curing for structural strength.

Methods of erecting these types of columns are explained on page 74.

### Steel posts

Impervious to fire, rot, and termite hazards, cylindrical steel posts offer exceptional structural strength in small dimensions—great for strong uncluttered deck substructures. One version is available with a concrete core for greater strength.

Because flanges for attaching the post to pier and beam must be welded to the ends, the posts must be cut to length and the welding done by a structural steel fabricator. This means extra care when installing concrete piers and estimating post heights—steel posts cannot be

adjusted on the job. They must be painted periodically for protection against rust.

### Steel substructures

The most costly deck substructure material is structural steel. It is used chiefly for high-level decks over steep downslopes of unstable soil and for decks connected to houses built on large steel-framed platforms. If you are considering a steel deck substructure, consult an architect or engineer on its design and construction.

### Deck foundations: Piers & footings

Most decks are anchored to the ground with foundations formed of piers and footings. Piers, made with metal connectors or wood blocks set in concrete (a combination of cement, sand, gravel, and water), provide support for the posts. Footings, also made of concrete, provide in-ground support for the piers.

Decks that aren't supported by the traditional concrete pier-and-footing arrangement may make use of wood posts treated for in-ground use. Wood posts, however, can be used only where ground is very stable and relatively dry.

## Concrete foundations

When using concrete, you can choose between mixing the concrete yourself (page 74) or buying it in one of the two forms listed below.

**Ready-made piers.** The work of forming piers can be eliminated if you buy readily available precast piers—and the cost is probably less than if you make them yourself. Precast piers, though, are usually available only with nailing blocks embedded for toenailing wood posts, the least secure method of post attachment. Bonding precast piers to footings is also less secure than forming and pouring piers and footings in one operation.

**Concrete blocks.** Excellent substitutes for precast piers are ordinary concrete building blocks with two or three core holes. Use the "standard aggregate" type rather than lightweight or "cinder" blocks. Nominal dimensions of full-size blocks are 8 by 8 by 16 inches or 8 by 12 by 16 inches. The core holes should be filled with concrete for added strength. Half-blocks, if available, allow you to build a pier as small as 8 by 8 inches.

## Wood post foundations

Wood posts—either foundation grade redwood, cedar, or cypress, or posts treated with preservatives for in-ground use—are an easy way to anchor decks to the ground. However, care must be taken to set them properly in very

firm soil on a footing of gravel, rock, or concrete.

## Hardware: Post attachments, metal connectors & nails

Building supply outlets carry an assortment of hardware used in deck construction, including post attachments and metal connectors that both simplify and strengthen construction.

### Post attachments

The strongest anchorages for wood posts are metal plate-and-pin-type fasteners that are embedded in piers or block core holes when the concrete is poured (see illustration below). Costs depend on type and

STRAP ANCHOR

NAILING BLOCK

CORNER ANGLE

DRIFT PIN

size. For pipe posts, you can make the same cast-in-place anchorages by putting long lag screws in floor flange screw holes and casting the setup like a plate-and-pin post fastener.

These post attachments are recommended for situations where building codes require extra-strong deck anchorage: timber substructures, high wind areas, heavy snow loads, and steep slopes. They should also be used for corner posts (and perhaps all posts) of freestand-

ing decks that have no structural ties to retaining walls or other firm support.

### Metal connectors

For strong, easy-to-form joints, a variety of metal straps, plates, angles, and hangers are available. Because these fasteners join more firmly than either toenailing or cleats, they are recommended for high-level decks expected to bear heavy loads or withstand high winds. Several types of metal connectors are illustrated below.

POST ANCHOR          BEAM TO POST

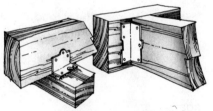
RIGHT ANGLE BRACKETS

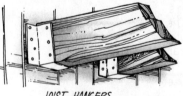
JOIST HANGERS

### Nails & other fastenings

To avoid unattractive nail stains or streaks on your deck, use noncorrosive nails and other fastenings (such as lag screws) for its construction. Top-quality, hot-dipped galvanized fastenings are unlikely to corrode in wet conditions or lose their power to hold. Stainless steel or aluminum alloy fastenings also are effective, though not easily available. To use nails, screws, and bolts, see charts on pages 93–94.

## Buyer's guide to decking lumber

Acquaint yourself with a few lumber terms and the characteristics of different wood species before you visit your lumberyard (see the chart "Comparative guide to lumber species," page 95). The lumber you use to build your deck is likely to take the largest slice of your project dollar, and it has a decided influence in the deck's finished appearance. Knowing a few conditions and trade terms will help you keep more dollars in your pocket without sacrificing quality.

### Lumber terms

Equipping yourself with a basic vocabulary of lumber terms can save you a good deal of time, trouble, and money when you pay a visit to the local lumberyard. Here are a few of the most important terms you should know:

**"Softwood" and "hardwood."** All woods are classified under one of these two categories. The terms do not refer to the relative hardness of woods but to the type of tree the woods come from: softwoods come from evergreens (conifers), hardwoods from broadleaf (deciduous) trees. Because hardwoods are generally more expensive and harder to work with, only softwoods are recommended for deck construction.

**"Nominal" and "surfaced" sizes.** Unless you buy logs, your lumber is sliced into boards of different sizes at the mill. The dimensions of these rough boards are the nominal sizes used to identify them: a "2 by 4" in its rough state is 2 inches thick by 4 inches wide. But lumber is almost always dried, causing it to shrink slightly, and then dressed by further planing to a "surfaced size." This is the size you actually get when ordering standard lumber. A 2 by 4 is not 2 inches by 4 inches unless it is left unseasoned and rough; you receive a board that

is actually 1½ inches by 3½ inches (unless you specify "rough"). The chart on page 94 shows nominal and surfaced sizes for standard lumber.

A surfaced board usually has all four of its sides planed smooth (designated "S4S").

*Board lumber* has nominal dimensions less than 2 inches in thickness and more than 2 inches in width.

*Dimension lumber* has nominal dimensions between 2 and 4 inches in thickness and more than 2 inches in width.

*Timber* is the term used to describe any lumber whose nominal thickness and width are both 5 inches or greater.

**"Heartwood" and "sapwood."** The inactive wood nearest the center of a living tree is called heartwood. Sapwood, next to the bark, contains the growth cells. Heartwood resists decay more efficiently; sapwood is more porous and absorbs preservatives and other chemicals better. One note of interest: cypress, cedar, and redwood heartwood are more resistant to decay and termites than other species.

**"Unseasoned," "dry," and "kiln-dried."** The moisture content of lumber dramatically affects shrinkage, nail-holding, and other important properties of wood (the greater its moisture content, the more likely it will be to split, warp, or cup as it dries). Lumber, either air-dried in stacks or kiln-dried, is marked according to its moisture content: S-GRN for "green," unseasoned lumber with moisture content of 20 percent or higher; S-DRY for lumber with a moisture content of 19 percent or less; and MC 15 for lumber dried to 15 percent (or less) moisture content. "Green" lumber requires further on-site seasoning before use.

**"Vertical" and "flat" grain.** Depending on the cut of the mill-saw, lumber will have either parallel grain lines running the length of the boards (vertical grain), or a marbled appearance (flat grain)—or a combination of the two (see illustration below). If you deck with flat-grain lumber, place boards bark-side up

(see page 80) to minimize grain separation, cupping, and splinters.

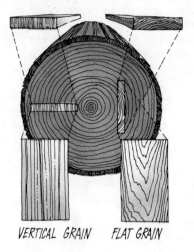

VERTICAL GRAIN    FLAT GRAIN

### Lumber grades

At the mill, lumber is sorted (a little like produce) into different grades, then identified with a stamp or inventoried according to species, quality, moisture content, and grade name.

Generally, lumber grading depends on natural growth characteristics, on defects resulting from milling errors, and on manufacturing techniques in drying and preserving that affect the strength, durability, or appearance of each board.

Natural imperfections in wood, illustrated below, include knots and shakes (cracks across the grain). Manufactured imperfections, produced during the milling process, include checks (cracks across the grain), splits, warp, and wane.

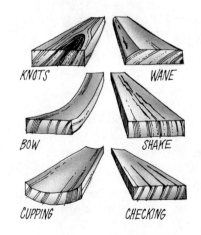

KNOTS    WANE

BOW    SHAKE

CUPPING    CHECKING

Naturally, the freer the board is from these blemishes, the higher will be its assigned grade—and the higher its price. The cost of a 2 by 4 of the finest grade, for example, may be two to three times the price of a medium quality 2 by 4 of the same length and species.

## Lumber preservatives

Any time untreated wood comes in contact with the ground or forms a joint that traps water, it will eventually rot and lose its strength. For this reason, many building codes require that wood structures coming within 6 inches of the ground be built either with woods that naturally resist decay (the foundation grades of cedar, redwood, or cypress), or less durable woods that have been pressure-treated with preservatives.

Wood preservatives—especially those applied commercially under pressure—extend the life of lumber by giving it a higher resistance to decay caused by fungi, mold, and wood-eating insects. Under pressure treatment, during which chemical preservatives are forced deep into wood fibers, lumber from species such as Southern pine or Douglas fir can be made as durable as the hardier types. Preservatives also can be applied with a brush or by immersion, but the long-term results are less satisfactory.

How much and which type of preservative a wood requires depends on the natural durability of the lumber species and its intended use. Generally, though, lumber used in foundations must have a higher resistance to decay than lumber used for deck surfaces. Lumber with low natural resistance to decay must be better protected than lumber that naturally withstands decay.

For more information on lumber preservatives and finishes, see pages 84–87, "Protecting your investment."

## How to keep your lumber costs down

Blemish-free decks built of blemish-free woods can price you right out of your project. On the other hand, using the lowest possible grades of wood (those with numerous knots, checks, and other imperfections) can produce a deck which, after 2 or 3 years, doesn't look a day under 50.

Since the cost of wood (particularly the durable, clear woods) will take the biggest bite out of your construction dollar, consider the following cost-curbing techniques:

• *Keep your deck design simple.* Complicated deck designs (they include decks with diagonal or checkerboard surfaces) often require complex support systems and, thus, more wood. Designing your deck to make the most of the least amount of wood can reduce your material costs substantially.

• *Work with standard dimensions.* Use lumber most commonly available—usually widths of 2 inches and lengths of 8, 10, 12, 14, and 16 feet—and design the deck to make maximum use of board lengths. For example, you can surface an 8-foot-wide deck with planks for the same cost as a deck that measures 7 feet 3 inches. Similarly, you will eliminate considerable waste if you trim a proposed deck from 14 feet 4 inches wide to 14 feet.

• *Use readily available kinds of wood.* The cost of lumber depends in part on how close to the market its species is logged; the kinds of lumber available locally also may depend on what grows in the nearby forests. Check local lumber outlets to find out what's available to you, what you can order, and what comparative costs are between available species and grades. Where appearance and physical properties are similar, choose the most economical species.

• *Combine lumber species.* It may be to your advantage to use different species of lumber for different parts of your deck. For example, a deck surfaced for appearance with a high-cost, clear grade of redwood or cedar may have a substructure built of lower-grade and less-costly Douglas fir. (Douglas fir, incidentally, often is preferred to other species as structural framing material because of its high strength.)

• *Try to buy wholesale.* When you begin to shop around for lumber prices, try to locate a wholesale lumber dealer who, though specializing in contractor sales, also sells at a retail level. Prices there are likely to be lower than those charged at building supply centers or other retail outlets that carry tools, hardware, and other building materials. And, if you can buy through a wholesaler/retailer, you also may have access to a wider range of lumber grades and species (see "Ordering materials," page 68).

## Deck kits & prefabricated decking

Complete deck kits (including standard designs and all materials for deck surfacing and substructure) are available from some lumberyards in various parts of the country. You also can buy prefabricated wood panels used for surfacing decks; they come in an assortment of rectangular sizes and generally include detailed plans of the beam and joist arrangements needed for support. Kits and preassembled decking do make construction simpler than "building from scratch," but they also increase materials costs.

Also aimed at the amateur home builder are deck design projects and idea literature developed by lumber associations. The California Redwood Association makes available a "Redwood Design-a-Deck" planning kit with building instructions and deck design ideas (send $5 with your request to The California Redwood Association, 1 Lombard Street, San Francisco, CA 94111). It also publishes an assortment of idea booklets for additional deck and garden projects, as well as information sheets dealing with lumber grades, uses, and finishes.

Western Wood Products Association (1500 Yeon Building, Portland, OR 97204) publishes a variety of pamphlets featuring do-it-yourself deck and garden projects; the pamphlets are available on request at nominal charges. Write for a list of publications.

# DRAWING A WORKABLE DECK DESIGN

### Information to help you:

- **produce a detailed plan for your deck**
- **plan for its topside features**
- **avoid costly construction errors**

Good design, in the case of decks, means that all the different parts—foundation, framework, and deck surface—work together in a structure that has the appearance you want and the sturdiness you need. Arriving at this goal requires that you coordinate the structural elements (see sketch below) so that the finished product suits your tastes and budget and meets local building requirements.

After you settle on a location for the deck and the materials you expect to use in its construction, concentrate first on the topside features, such as the surface, steps, railings, and other elements that stand out visually. Then design (or have a professional design) the supporting substructure and foundation.

The following pages are your introduction to the specifications and techniques necessary to design a wood deck. As you work, you may wish to refer to the chapter "Building Your Deck" (pages 70–83) for help in drawing parts of your deck in detail.

The simplest and most economical decks to build are those with squared-off sides. Curved decks are possible, though they usually require more complex support systems. Multilevel decks connected by steps, stairs, or ramps require more work than single-level decks.

### Structural view of a deck

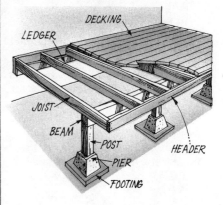

### Tips for drawing plans

To draw deck plans, you need graph paper with 8 squares to

the inch, plus a ruler, a couple of medium pencils, and an eraser. To determine dimensions and grade levels on the construction site, you also need a tape measure (a 50-foot tape is most convenient), a carpenter's level or line level, mason's twine, and a supply of 1 by 2 or 2 by 2 stakes, each about 18 inches long and pointed at one end. Use your scale drawing (see page 9) as a reference.

## Plan & elevation views

A deck's basic surface pattern and substructure should be drawn in *plan* views (seen from above looking straight down). Arrangement of the substructure, railings, and other vertical members should be drawn in *elevation* views (seen straight-on from one side). Attachments and other details should be drawn from the view that most clearly shows their construction.

## Drawing to scale

The scale of a drawing is the number of inches or feet represented by each square on the graph paper. Generally, the more squares used to represent 1 foot or 1 inch of actual deck dimensions, the more precise and useful your plans will be.

A scale in which 6 squares equal 1 foot (6:1) works well for deck surfacing patterns and general arrangements of joists, beams, and posts. In the 6:1 scale, 1 square equals 2 inches. However, a scale larger than 6:1 should be used for details of railings, benches, and other relatively small features. For these, the easiest scale to work with is 1 square equaling 1 inch. Tape several sheets of graph paper together if you need a larger drawing area than one sheet.

## Designing the deck surface

Because deck-surfacing materials such as tile and concrete are best laid with the aid of a professional, and because the installation of other materials may vary with each manufacturer, design suggestions given here deal only with wooden decking materials.

## Patterns for dimension lumber

As the drawing below indicates, you can lay decking lumber perpendicular or diagonal to the joists (or to beams, if joists are not used), or in several variations, as long as you provide support under each end of each piece. Generally speaking, the more complex the deck pattern, the more complicated the substructure must be.

You will eliminate unnecessary waste and on-site cutting if you design your deck so that it can be surfaced with lumber in readily available standard lengths of 8, 12, 16, 20 (redwood's maximum length), or 24 feet. Decking lumber should be spaced slightly to allow for drainage, ventilation, and expansion and contraction of the wood. Commonest spacing is 3/16 inch. Narrower spacings between lumber tend to trap decaying leaves and other litter that can be troublesome to extract. Wider spacing allows small items such as utensils to slip through the deck, high heels to catch between planks.

**Standard parallel patterns.** The simplest, soundest, and most economical decking patterns are those made of 2 by 4 or 2 by 6 lumber laid parallel and spaced, running the full length or width of the deck.

Whether the decking runs across the length or width depends on the deck's substructure; decking should be laid perpendicular to joists (or to beams, if the design does not call for joists). For example, when a deck attached to a house uses a ledger attached to a wall as a support for joists, the joists run perpendicular to that wall, so the decking must be parallel or diagonal to the wall regardless of dimension. On the other hand, low-level decks without joists usually have beams running the deck's long axis; the decking then lies at right angles to the beams, across the deck's width.

**Varying lumber widths.** The simplest variations of parallel deck patterns make use of two or more different widths of 2-inch dimen-

## Eight designs for surface patterns

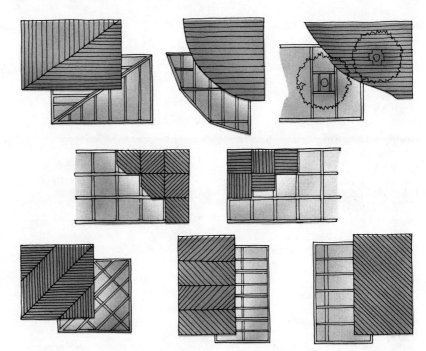

sion lumber. Many combinations are possible; several are illustrated below.

### Parallel deck patterns

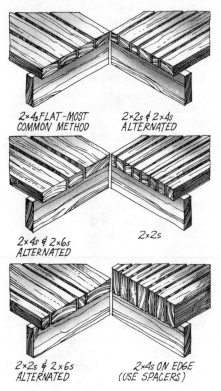

2×4s FLAT-MOST COMMON METHOD

2×2s & 2×4s ALTERNATED

2×4s & 2×6s ALTERNATED

2×2s

2×2s & 2×6s ALTERNATED

2×4s ON EDGE (USE SPACERS)

"On-edge" patterns are created when 2 by 3s or 2 by 4s are laid on their sides (on edge), usually directly on beams. On-edge decking is expensive and heavy but can span long distances between supports—an advantage if you want to eliminate the clutter of joists in a high-level deck, or if you want to keep a simple substructure under a low-level deck.

**Diagonal decking.** If you intend to lay dimension lumber diagonally over the substructure, design the beams or joists closer than normal, because a plank laid diagonally must span a greater distance than the same board laid perpendicular to its support. Board ends can be trimmed to a complementary angle to make them flush with the house wall.

**Checkerboard patterns.** To create a checkerboard effect, divide the total deck area into equal squares and then surface the squares in alternating directions.

The deck must be rectangular or square and the checkerboard modules at least 3 feet but not more than 4 feet square. Multiples of four are simplest to work with. However, if your deck dimensions are in odd feet or feet plus inches —for example, 11 feet 7 inches by 19 feet 3 inches—convert the dimensions to inches and divide into equal squares. Keep in mind that support spacings also must correspond evenly to the squares' dimensions; blocking between joists or beams will be necessary for support under every end of every piece of surface lumber.

### Subflooring

To design either a tongue-and-groove or plywood subfloor for a deck surfaced with rubberized coatings, ceramic or clay tiles, or vinyl, sandwich a layer of overlapped building paper (15-pound asphalt felt) between two wood surfaces, as the illustration below indicates. And if you use boards, run the top boards either at right or 45° angles to the lower ones. If using mortar or concrete, plan to add another layer of builder's paper or polyethylene sheeting over the top layer of wood.

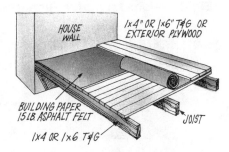

HOUSE WALL

1×4" OR 1×6" T&G OR EXTERIOR PLYWOOD

BUILDING PAPER 15 LB ASPHALT FELT

JOIST

1×4 OR 1×6 T&G

### Tongue-&-groove subfloors.
Tongue-and-groove boards are laid like dimension lumber but without the spacing. Decks with these boards should be designed with a slight slope to allow adequate drainage, and you should plan to seal the lumber with a waterproof coating.

**Plywood subfloors.** Two considerations are important when designing with plywood as a deck subfloor. First, be certain that the plywood is thick enough to span

spaces between joists or beams without bowing. The usual choice is ¾-inch, though thicker plywood with T&G edges can eliminate the need for joists. Second, make sure that all square edges are supported either by a beam, a joist, or blocking between beams or joists. Blocking may be omitted when plywood is milled with T&G edges.

## Designing the substructure

With your deck surface drawn in plan view, you are ready to design the deck's supporting framework. In the tables that follow are specifications for different arrangements of the substructure's joists, beams, and posts.

### Deck loads & heights

Building codes in many areas require a substructure to be strong enough to support 40 pounds of "live" load per square foot, plus 10 pounds of "dead" weight. The tables and other design information are based on this "40 plus 10 p.s.f." loading at deck heights up to 12 feet.

Decks higher than 12 feet above grade (even at only one post), or decks that must bear heavy snow loads or large planters may require cross bracing and stronger posts —designs best left to a structural engineer or other professional.

### Allowable spans & spacings

A span is the distance deck planks, joists, or beams must bridge; spacing is the distance between joist and joist, beam and beam, or post and post (see illustration on next page). Both are critically important to proper substructure design, because they determine the ultimate strength or weakness of the support system. A deck with joists spaced too far apart will simply sag beneath your weight and feel oddly elastic underfoot.

The maximum safe spans and spacings for lumber of different dimensions depend on the wood species and grade you plan to use in the deck's construction.

## Deck spans & spacings

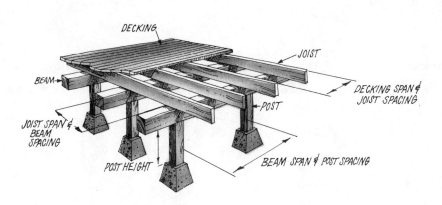

DECKING

JOIST

DECKING SPAN & JOIST SPACING

BEAM

POST

JOIST SPAN & BEAM SPACING

POST HEIGHT

BEAM SPAN & POST SPACING

### How to use the tables

Use the five tables that follow to find the proper sizes, spans, spacings, and heights for the substructure elements. As you work through them, you'll find that you can create a number of equally effective joist-beam-post combinations, some more economical and attractive than others. Before you settle on one design, compare its cost and appearance against several other possibilities—and be sure the size lumber you want is available.

Also keep these points in mind:
• These tables are developed from the Uniform Building Code (UBC) and other sources that may not meet all local code requirements. Use them for planning and design, but also check with your building department.

• All beam and post dimensions are for sawed lumber, such as a 4 by 6 that measures 3½ by 5½ inches after surfacing. You cannot build an equally strong beam by sandwiching two 2 by 6s, because they measure only 3 (2 times 1½ inches) by 5½ inches.

• As you work out spans, spacings, and post heights, remember that those given in the tables are *maximum* limits. You can always choose shorter spans, closer spacings, or larger joists, beams, and posts.

**Table 1: Strength groupings of common softwoods.** Start your design with Table 1 to find the strength grouping of the wood species you plan to use in construction. These groupings include lumber

species graded No. 1 or better and are based on each species' bending strength, stiffness, and ability to withstand compression. (You may find it more economical to use different species of lumber for different parts of the deck; for example, if you've decided on redwood for the surface, you may want to use Douglas fir for the substructure.)

**Table 2: Choosing decking spans.** Next, using information from Table 1, work out the maximum spacing you can use between joists, or between beams if your design eliminates joists. Spacing between joists and beams depends on the maximum allowable span for your choice of decking. You have the option of designing a deck without joists by using more beams (useful if you want a low, ground-hugging deck or an uncluttered substructure), though more beams mean more posts and piers. Compare costs before you decide.

**Table 3: Maximum joist spans & spacings.** Next, use the information you've gathered from Tables 1 and 2 to determine the correct size and length of joists for the spacings determined in Table 2.

**Table 4: Beam sizes & spans.** The joist length from Table 3 or decking span from Table 2 determines spacing between the beams. The choices you have in beam spacing may be limited by the lumber sizes available.

**Table 5: Minimum post sizes.** To determine the post size from

Table 5, you need to know the strength group of wood for the posts (Table 1), the beam spacing (Table 4), and the post spacing. (The post spacing is identical to the beam span established in Table 4.) Multiply the beam spacing (in feet) by the post spacing (in feet) to determine the load area that each post supports. Then, from Table 5, select a post size that meets your height requirements. If you have a choice, choose a post with the same thickness as the beam—it will simplify construction.

### Bracing

Keep in mind that, despite the inherent strength in a deck's basic members, bracing is normally used to provide lateral stability and to help distribute loads evenly. See page 79 for information on bracing for joists (bridging) and for posts.

## Foundations

The deck foundation has two parts—concrete piers and footings (or their equivalents)—and three functions: 1) it anchors the substructure against settling, slippage, and wind lift; 2) it distributes the weight and deck loads into the ground; and 3), it protects posts from coming in direct contact with earth.

Almost all decks are supported by this basic foundation arrangement, one that most building codes require.

### Footings

A footing should be about twice the width of the pier or masonry it supports. Many communities specify surface dimensions of footings because they have to bear the deck's weight without cracking. Most also specify how far into the ground footings must extend—usually down to solid soil or rock and, in cold country, below the frost line so the soil doesn't heave and lift the footings.

These requirements are imposed for a good reason: footings that settle or slip out of their original positions can cause the substructure to twist or collapse.

## Specifications: Deck Spans & Spacings

### Table 1: Strength Groupings of Common Softwoods Species
(All groups are grade no. 1 or better.)

#### Group A
Douglas fir
Hemlock, Western
Larch, Western
Pine, Southern
Spruce, coast Sitka

#### Group B
Cedar, Western
Douglas fir (south)
Fir (white, Alpine)
Hemlock (Eastern, mountain)
Pine (Eastern white, Idaho white, lodgepole, Northern, Ponderosa, red, sugar, Western white)
Redwood
Spruce (Eastern, Engelmann, Sitka)

#### Group C
Cedar, Northern white

### Table 2: Choosing Decking Spans
(Dimension and board lumber)

| Decking Size & Type | Species Group | Maximum Span (inches) |
|---|---|---|
| 1 by 4s and 1 by 6s laid flat (S4S, T&G, and shiplap) | A | 16 |
| | B | 14 |
| | C | 12 |
| All 2-inch lumber widths laid flat (standard and T&G) | A | 64 |
| | B | 57 |
| | C | 51 |
| 2 by 3s laid on edge (standard lumber) | A | 108 |
| | B | 96 |
| | C | 86 |
| 2 by 4s laid on edge (standard lumber) | A | 152 |
| | B | 134 |
| | C | 120 |

Plywood: Maximum span depends on thickness, wood species from which constructed, and plywood grade. Exterior types used for decking are marked with an identification number. The digits behind the slash indicate maximum span in inches. Thus, a panel marked 48/24 can span 24 inches.

### Table 3: Maximum Joist Spans & Spacings

| Joist Size | Species Group | Maximum Span |
|---|---|---|
| **For 16-inch joist spacings:** | | |
| 2 by 6 | A | 9' 9" |
| | B | 8' 7" |
| | C | 7' 9" |
| 2 by 8 | A | 12' 10" |
| | B | 11' 4" |
| | C | 10' 2" |
| 2 by 10 | A | 16' 5" |
| | B | 14' 6" |
| | C | 13' 0" |
| **For 24-inch joist spacings:** | | |
| 2 by 6 | A | 8' 6" |
| | B | 7' 6" |
| | C | 6' 9" |
| 2 by 8 | A | 11' 3" |
| | B | 9' 11" |
| | C | 8' 11" |
| 2 by 10 | A | 14' 4" |
| | B | 12' 8" |
| | C | 11' 4" |
| **For 32-inch joist spacings:** | | |
| 2 by 6 | A | 7' 9" |
| | B | 6' 10" |
| | C | 6' 2" |
| 2 by 8 | A | 10' 2" |
| | B | 9' 0" |
| | C | 8' 1" |
| 2 by 10 | A | 13' 0" |
| | B | 11' 6" |
| | C | 10' 4" |

## Table 4: Beam Sizes & Spans

Beams are on edge. Spans are center-to-center distances between posts or supports.

**Spacing between beams (feet)**

### Species Group A (Table 1)

| Beam Size (inches) | 4 | 5 | 6 | 7 | 8 | 9 | 10 | 11 | 12 |
|---|---|---|---|---|---|---|---|---|---|
| 4 by 6 | up to 8' spans | up to 7' → | | up to 6' → | | | | (shaded) | |
| 3 by 8 | up to 9' → | | up to 8' → | | up to 7' → | | | up to 6' → | |
| 4 by 8 | up to 11' | up to 10' | up to 9' → | | up to 8' → | | | up to 7' → | |
| 3 by 10 | up to 12' | up to 11' → | | up to 10' → | | up to 9' → | | | up to 8' |
| 4 by 10 | up to 14' | up to 13' | up to 12' | up to 11' → | | up to 10' → | | | up to 9' |
| 3 by 12 | (shaded) | up to 14' | up to 13' | up to 12' → | | up to 11' → | | up to 10' → | |
| 4 by 12 | (shaded) | (shaded) | up to 14' → | | up to 13' → | | up to 12' → | | up to 11' |
| 6 by 10 | (shaded) | up to 14' → | | up to 13' → | | up to 12' → | | up to 11' → | |
| 6 by 12 | (shaded) | | | | | | up to 14' → | | up to 13' |

### Species Group B (Table 1)

| Beam Size (inches) | 4 | 5 | 6 | 7 | 8 | 9 | 10 | 11 | 12 |
|---|---|---|---|---|---|---|---|---|---|
| 4 by 6 | up to 7' spans | up to 6' → | | | (shaded) | | | | |
| 3 by 8 | up to 8' → | | up to 7' → | | up to 6' → | | | | |
| 4 by 8 | up to 9' → | | up to 8' → | | up to 7' → | | | up to 6' → | |
| 3 by 10 | up to 11' | up to 10' | up to 9' → | | up to 8' → | | | up to 7' → | |
| 4 by 10 | up to 12' | up to 11' | up to 10' → | | up to 9' → | | | up to 8' → | |
| 3 by 12 | up to 13' | up to 12' | up to 11' → | | up to 10' → | up to 9' → | | | |
| 4 by 12 | (shaded) | up to 14' | up to 13' | up to 12' | up to 11' → | | | up to 10' → | |
| 6 by 10 | up to 14' | up to 13' | up to 12' | up to 11' → | | | up to 10' → | | |
| 6 by 12 | (shaded) | | | up to 14' → | | up to 13' | up to 12' → | | |

### Species Group C (Table 1)

| Beam Size (inches) | 4 | 5 | 6 | 7 | 8 | 9 | 10 | 11 | 12 |
|---|---|---|---|---|---|---|---|---|---|
| 4 by 6 | up to 6' spans | (shaded) | | | | | | | |
| 3 by 8 | up to 7' → | | up to 6' → | | | (shaded) | | | |
| 4 by 8 | up to 8' → | | up to 7' → | up to 6' → | | | | | |
| 3 by 10 | up to 9' → | | up to 8' → | up to 7' → | | | | | (shaded) |
| 4 by 10 | up to 11' | up to 10' | up to 9' → | | up to 8' → | | | | |
| 3 by 12 | up to 12' | up to 11' | up to 10' → | | up to 9' → | | up to 8' → | | |
| 4 by 12 | up to 13' | up to 12' | up to 11' → | | up to 10' → | | up to 9' → | | |
| 6 by 10 | up to 12' → | | | up to 11' | up to 10' → | | up to 9' → | | up to 8' |
| 6 by 12 | (shaded) | up to 14' | up to 13' → | | up to 12' → | | up to 11' → | | up to 10' |

## Table 5: Post Sizes & Heights (Wood beams)

**Load area = beam spacing x post spacing (square feet)**

### Species Group A (Table 1)

| Post Size (inches) | 36 | 48 | 60 | 72 | 84 | 96 | 108 | 120 | 132 | 144 |
|---|---|---|---|---|---|---|---|---|---|---|
| 4 by 4 | up to 12' heights → | | | | up to 10' → | | | up to 8' → | | |
| 4 by 6 | (shaded) | | | | up to 12' → | | | up to 10' → | | |
| 6 by 6 | (shaded) | | | | | | | | up to 12' → | |

### Species Group B (Table 1)

| Post Size (inches) | 36 | 48 | 60 | 72 | 84 | 96 | 108 | 120 | 132 | 144 |
|---|---|---|---|---|---|---|---|---|---|---|
| 4 by 4 | up to 12' → | | up to 10' → | | up to 8' → | | | up to 6' → | | |
| 4 by 6 | (shaded) | | up to 12' → | | up to 10' → | | | up to 8' → | | |
| 6 by 6 | (shaded) | | | | | | up to 12' → | | | |

### Species Group C (Table 1)

| Post Size (inches) | 36 | 48 | 60 | 72 | 84 | 96 | 108 | 120 | 132 | 144 |
|---|---|---|---|---|---|---|---|---|---|---|
| 4 by 4 | up to 12' | up to 10' | up to 8' → | | up to 6' → | | | | | |
| 4 by 6 | up to 12' | up to 10' → | | up to 8' → | | | | up to 6' → | | |
| 6 by 6 | (shaded) | | up to 12' → | | | | | | | |

## Piers

Concrete piers may be cylindrical, rectangular, or pyramidal with flat tops. In all cases—with or without footings—they must have a top surface large enough to hold nailing blocks or other post attachment devices with room to spare. In place, piers should be exposed at least 6 inches above earth. See page 19 for information on ready-made piers; to pour your own, see page 74.

## Railings, benches, screens & overheads

Plan for railings, benches, screens, and overheads before you finish the deck. All of these topside features should be securely connected to the deck's substructure and must be considered with the deck's initial design.

You have a framework for designing these supplementary deck features in local building codes and the architectural style of your house. Building codes, for example, will tell you how high railings must be (usually 36 inches if the deck sits higher than 30 inches above grade) and how high screens and overheads can be. And the architectural style of your house will help you choose materials appropriate to your setting.

### Posts to support topside features

Vertical posts are the supports for topside structures, and they differ only in size, height, and numbers required by a specific design.

The sturdiest post arrangement is simply to extend the main posts of the deck's substructure through the deck surface and to the proper height (see illustration at right).

If posts aren't in the right location for your topside design, fasten railing posts and bench supports to deck beams, joists, or headers. Secure screen and overhead posts to beams only (see sketch far right).

### Railing & screen designs

Design variations for railings and screens are virtually unlimited.

They can have rails, pickets, louvers, or any number of solid facings such as shingles, siding, stucco, plastic panels, or tempered glass. Those designed with rails can be built with anything from standard 2 by 4s to decorative lathe-turned posts to wrought iron.

**Basic structure.** Regardless of design, railings and screens have the same basic structure: vertical posts capped and joined by a cross member laid flat. The cross member—either the same width or wider than the posts—should completely cover the post ends.

Spacing between the posts depends on the size of the cap and the lengths of the horizontal rails, though generally posts can be spaced up to 4 feet apart under a 2 by 4 cap and up to 6 feet apart under a 2 by 6. (Screens of this basic structure should not be higher than 8 feet.)

Details of six typical railing and screen designs are illustrated on the next page. Variations should follow these same general rules. Sketch a number of designs before you make a final choice.

**Rail-to-post connections.** The strongest and simplest railings or screens are those whose horizontal members are nailed to the outside faces of the posts. You can get a cleaner, more streamlined railing, though, if you place horizontals

between the posts. Fastening techniques are illustrated below. Two common fastening techniques are *not* recommended: simple toenailed joints (they aren't strong enough) and dado or mortised joints (they collect decay-causing moisture).

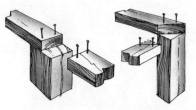

BUTT JOINT       MITRE AT CORNER

CLEAT AND METAL FASTENINGS

### Benches

Benches are almost indispensable if a finished deck is to be useful. Besides providing seating, they can funnel foot traffic, separate areas for different activities, provide railings for low-level decks (and for high-level decks if they have backs), and serve as sun-

## For topside features: Two ways to attach posts

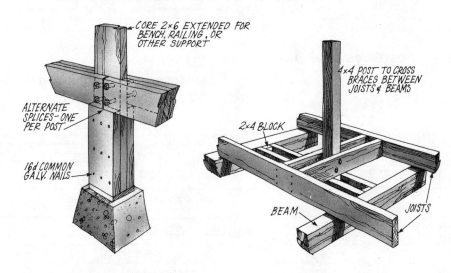

CORE 2×6 EXTENDED FOR BENCH, RAILING, OR OTHER SUPPORT

ALTERNATE SPLICES—ONE PER POST

16d COMMON GALV. NAILS

4×4 POST TO CROSS BRACES BETWEEN JOISTS & BEAMS

2×4 BLOCK

BEAM

JOISTS

## Six railing & screen designs

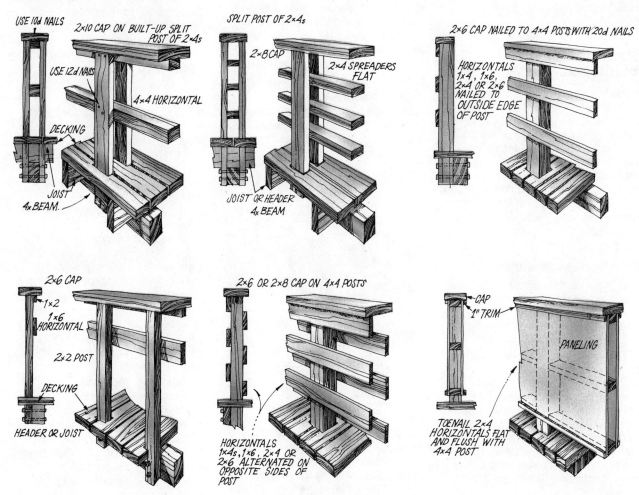

USE 10d NAILS

2×10 CAP ON BUILT-UP SPLIT POST OF 2×4s

USE 12d NAILS

4×4 HORIZONTAL

DECKING

JOIST
4× BEAM

SPLIT POST OF 2×4s

2×8 CAP

2×4 SPREADERS FLAT

JOIST OR HEADER
4× BEAM

2×6 CAP NAILED TO 4×4 POSTS WITH 20d NAILS

HORIZONTALS
1×4, 1×6,
2×4 OR 2×6
NAILED TO
OUTSIDE EDGE
OF POST

2×6 CAP

1×2

1×6
HORIZONTAL

2×2 POST

DECKING

HEADER OR JOIST

2×6 OR 2×8 CAP ON 4×4 POSTS

HORIZONTALS
1×4s, 1×6, 2×4 OR
2×6 ALTERNATED ON
OPPOSITE SIDES OF
POST

CAP

1" TRIM

PANELING

TOENAIL 2×4
HORIZONTALS FLAT
AND FLUSH WITH
4×4 POST

LEAVE ABOUT 1½" BETWEEN BOTTOM HORIZONTAL AND DECKING FOR DRAINAGE

bathing lounges, tables, and plant display platforms.

For conventional seating, a bench should be between 15 and 18 inches high. (Sunbathing platforms may be as low as 6 to 8 inches.) Backs on chair-height benches should provide support at least 12 inches above the seat; the seat itself should be at least 15 inches deep. Backs of deck benches can be capped like railings; caps protect post ends from decay and, when level, provide surfaces for food and drinks.

## Overheads

Overheads above decks are essentially patio roofs. They can be designed to filter light, provide protection from rain, or simply add to the intimacy and esthetics of the deck. Wood, plastic, glass, and fabrics all may be used in overhead construction.

The supporting framework of most overheads is similar to the deck's substructure, but lighter; 30 pounds per square foot loading usually meets legal requirements in mild snowfall areas. Rafters are equivalent to joists; beams, ledgers, and posts serve the same purpose for both decks and overheads (see illustration at right).

Build an overhead as you would a deck; spans of the beams and joists in the tables (pages 26–27) usually can be increased by as much as 1 foot.

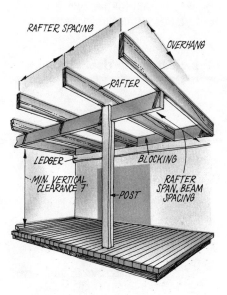

RAFTER SPACING

OVERHANG

RAFTER

LEDGER

BLOCKING

MIN. VERTICAL
CLEARANCE 7'

POST

RAFTER
SPAN, BEAM
SPACING

For detailed information on patio roofs, see the *Sunset* book *How to Build Patio Roofs.*

## Steps, ramps & multilevels

Aside from serving as simple access, steps, ramps, and graduated deck levels also can be used to set traffic patterns, dramatize a deck area or the house, eliminate the need for extensive site grading, and provide additional seating. Whatever their purpose, their dimensions should fall in line with specific rules combining safety, usefulness, and esthetics.

### Rise & passage width

*Rise* is the vertical distance between adjacent surfaces of different levels. *Passage width* is the usable area between the sides of a stair or ramp.

The width of steps, stairs, and ramps should be based on the following minimums for general access: provide at least 4 feet for one person, 5 feet for two abreast; add 2 feet per person for greater numbers of side-by-side users. Service stairs or other deliberately restricted access may have a minimum passage width of 2 feet.

### Steps & stairs

Steps and stairs that lead from a deck generally fall into one of three categories: *straight-run* steps that move directly from one level to another without interruption; *L-type* steps that make a single right-angle turn; and *U-type* stairs that reverse themselves in a 180° turn at a landing. Most home carpenters should restrict their efforts to straight-run steps.

### Treads, risers & stringers.

Horizontal *treads* and vertical *risers* supported by *stringers* are the basic parts of steps and stairs (see sketch below).

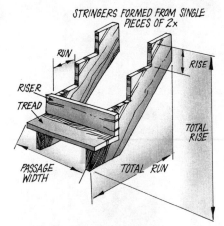

For steps to be safe and comfortable to use, the tread width and riser height must maintain a particular relationship (see illustration below). For outdoor steps, twice the riser height added to the tread width should equal 26 inches. When figuring tread dimensions, measure the tread from riser to riser and disregard any overhang.

Both ends of stringers must be firmly anchored either to another structure or to concrete footings (see page 80).

**Ground-to-deck access.** High-level and low-level decks have different deck-to-ground relationships that require different types of access routes.

For example, the main access on a hillside deck is usually through the house; narrow flights of unobtrusive stairs may provide adequate access to the yard below. (If the rise is higher than 8 feet, a U-type flight of stairs with a midway landing will be less conspicuous.)

At deck heights less than 8 feet above grade, the type of deck-to-ground access changes and the deck itself is often the main route between house and garden. It calls for wide passages and single-flight steps with moderate tread-to-riser ratios. Normally, ramps are unsuitable because of the extreme length (30 to 35 feet for a 4-foot deck) needed to obtain a comfortable walking slope.

Low-level decks less than a foot or two above grade tie nicely into a garden scheme, especially when deck-wide steps or ramps are used to connect structure and garden. Steps running the full length or width of a deck also serve to hide views of the support structure. Whether steps or ramps extend the deck's full length or only part of it, all passage widths should be generous: for steps, keep risers low (4 or 4½ inches) and treads wide (17 or 18 inches) to produce a smooth transition.

**How to measure for steps.** To determine the number of steps you need, measure the vertical distance from the deck to the ground; then divide by the riser height, say 6½ inches. (For example, if the deck is 45½ inches above grade, 45½ ÷ 6½ = 7 steps exactly.) If the answer for the number of steps ends in a fraction, divide the whole number into the vertical distance to learn the exact measurement for each riser. (If the deck is 54 inches above grade, 54 ÷ 6½ = 8+ steps; 54 ÷ 8 = 6¾ inches rise per step.)

Next, subtract twice the exact riser height from the maximum tread

### Typical tread-to-riser ratios

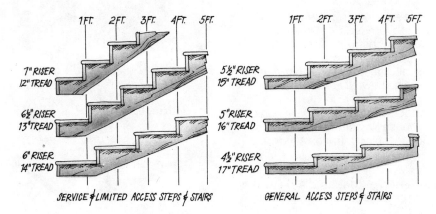

depth, 26 inches, to find the proper depth of each tread (26 − 13 = 13). No tread should be less than 11 inches and no riser more than 7½ inches.

Finally, determine the "total run" —horizontal distance between top and bottom risers—to find out whether your plan will fit available space. Multiply the tread depth by the number of risers minus one (in the example, 6 × 13 = 78); if the steps don't fit, make adjustments in the riser-tread relationship, increasing one and decreasing the other.

## Ramps

Relatively easy to build, ramps are useful for deck access where the rise is less than 3 feet (the ramp's length may be a drawback for higher rises).

A simple ramp is made from the same material as the deck and is supported by two or more 4 by 4 stringers. Stringers are attached to deck joists, facers, or substructure members by the same methods illustrated for stairs on page 80.

**Measuring for ramps.** The length of the ramp determines its slope. To find the shortest length for a comfortable walking slope, simply multiply the height of the rise by 8. You may always use a longer ramp, but a shorter one will be too steep for general deck access. One tip: Be sure to measure the rise from the top surface of the deck surface to the top surface of the second deck or to the ground. Design ramps so that all meeting surfaces are flush to eliminate tripping.

## Changing deck levels

Whether by design or necessity, decks are frequently built on two levels. Sometimes the second level is simply a narrow walkway, sometimes it serves as a secondary deck surface.

**Design considerations.** Deck levels separated by more than 4½ inches of rise should be joined by steps or a ramp. For rises greater than 8 inches, steps are usually

more practical than ramps because they consume less space.

You can design steps or ramps to be as wide as the deck surface they join; or you can restrict passage between levels by designing one or two sets of narrow steps separated by benches. Steps with 19 to 28-inch treads can dramatize a mid-deck change of levels.

**Two ways to change levels.**
An easy way to change deck levels is to first build the deck's lower level (see sketch below left), then add a ledger to beam and joists. Joists of the upper level will rest on the ledger. Decking overhangs a 2-inch facer board.

For a more distinct level change, tie the joists of the lower level to the first rank of posts of the upper level, as the illustration below right indicates. In the interest of safety, cover the gap with decking or other sturdy material.

## Hand railings

The rise height and passage width are important factors in deciding the need for railing on steps, stairs, and ramps. Passage widths of 8 feet or more seldom require railings, even though the rise may be several feet. On the other hand, stairs and ramps with passage widths of 4 or 5 feet almost always need railings, regardless of the rise height, for reasons of both psychology and safety. Also good candidates for railings are some

long ramps that appear narrow because of their extreme length.

**Design requirements.** Generally, railings on stairs and ramps must meet the same design requirements as deck perimeter railings described on page 28. Minimum heights are 30 inches, and maximum heights are 34 inches from top of railing to the top front edges of the treads. Posts should be bolted or lag-screwed to the stringers, never to the stair treads or ramp surface. Caps (bannisters) should cover the tops of posts.

The major difference between deck perimeter railings and stair or ramp railings is that any cross members between posts must parallel the slope or the stair or ramp stringers (see below). The design

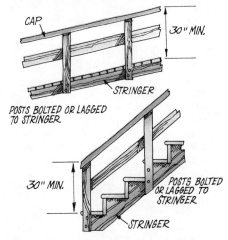

of deck perimeter railings, however, usually can be adapted for stair and ramp railings.

### Two ways to change deck levels

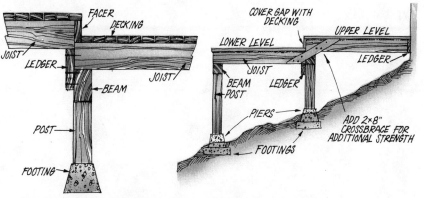

***For moderate level change*** *(left), first build lower level, then add a ledger to beam and joist. For major level change (right), first build upper level. Lower-level joists rest on ledger added to outside of upper post and beams.*

# DECK IDEAS IN COLOR

To spark your own inspiration, browse through this color wheel of deck ideas, including:

- imaginative entries
- ground-level & hillside sites
- small spaces & narrow lots
- benches & railings

Whatever the size and shape of your lot, decking lumber makes it possible to turn that "same old yard" into your home's most versatile room. As an out-of-doors room of your own, the deck might offer a secluded getaway spot for reading or simply lounging under the warm rays of the sun. As a room to share with family and friends, perhaps it's the place where kids can battle out a round of Monopoly, or where good friends can gather for supper on a summer's eve.

Let the ideas in the following pages be a springboard to the outdoor living area you want. The decks shown in this chapter range from tiny tuck-away decks for pocket gardens to grand-scale entertainment areas with sweeping panoramas. Architecturally, they vary from the best of traditional to eye-catching contemporary. They have been designed to suit places both hilly and pancake flat, or—as in the case of the roof decks pictured on pages 60–61—whatever structural settings are available.

As you browse through this section, focus your attention on the functions you want your deck to serve—private garden sitting spot? outdoor play space for children? adult entertainment center? open-air dining room? Then see which deck ideas can best be tailored to your own situation. And in designing, keep one eye on simplicity, for simplicity in design is the backbone of outdoor rooms with lasting appeal and comfort.

*Low-level bridges* link three outdoor living areas and help to break up space in a narrow, wedge-shaped yard. Garden plan and more photographs are on page 47. Design: Robert S. Rubel.

*Enclosed courtyard,* reached through a trellis-covered gate, doubles as a private sitting spot for condominium owners. To provide a level surface and a warmer feeling, decking was laid over an existing sloped concrete patio. Raised beds of brick (see plan below) accent both ends of garden. Design: William Louis Kapranos.

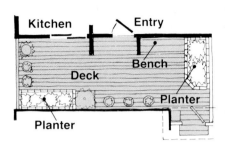

# FITTING FIRST IMPRESSIONS: ENTRY DECKS THAT SAY "WELCOME"

**Two decks are bridges, the third a walled court**

**Bridging a sloping site,** *redwood entry deck provides a level approach to front door. Surfaced with alternating 2 by 2s and 2 by 6s, deck floats over a low-maintenance rock garden. Tall posts support streetlamplike lights; balusters are beveled at top for a sophisticated, finished look. Design: Ron Yeo.*

**Charming entry deck** *takes you to front door, or two steps up to kitchen door (at left), or past kitchen to an upper level carport. Deck surface was left to weather naturally, but railings were painted to match house siding. In one spot a shading oak grows right through railing. Design: Henry Blackard.*

# STREETSIDE DECKS DESIGNED FOR PRIVACY

## The trick is to create a barrier without a sense of confinement

**Surrounded by solid cedar fencing** and a roof-high screen, streetside deck gets plenty of privacy and lots of morning sun. Deck, raised two steps above a brick path, is located off dining room (see plan above) and alongside a small entry deck. Shapes of decks add angular composition to a rectangular yard. Design: Robert W. Chittock.

**Handsome, patterned deck** *(above)
replaced an existing concrete porch
and changed the face of a once-bland
entry. Now an outdoor sitting spot
as well as an entry (right), deck is
protected from street views by a
screen made of prestained redwood
1 by 1s, lath, and benderboard. (See
plan below.) Design: Donald G. Boos.*

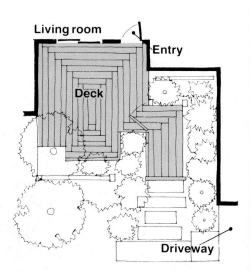

Living room

Entry

Deck

Driveway

# GARDEN FLOORS PAVED WITH GROUND-HUGGING DECKS

## . . . like having another room in the house

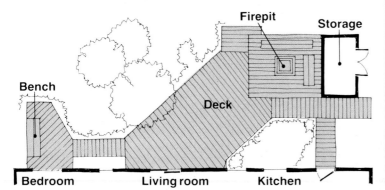

**Angular fir deck** *stretches through a spacious yard to make room for a gamut of family activities. Main deck easily accommodates kids' toys and games; raised platform is a barbecue center (see plan above). Walk in foreground leads to a sitting area off master bedroom. Design: Bennett, Johnson, Slenes & Smith.*

**Just three short steps from the dock,** *simple platform deck squeezes into a small back yard to take advantage of a waterfront setting. Built of redwood, the deck measures only 12 by 14 feet but seems larger because of simple parallel decking pattern and built-in seating. Design: John and Anne Kelley.*

*You don't have to go far* for a picnic in this yard—for the zigzag benches and picnic table provide plenty of room for alfresco meals. Built over an existing concrete patio, deck and bench were designed to accommodate a hot tub and prized Japanese black pine. Tub becomes a table when owners cover it with a wooden lid. Design: Ed Hoiland.

*Where levels change,* decking changes direction in this low-level deck designed for a small, wedge-shaped yard. Bordered by beds of blooming agapanthus and sweet alyssum, deck makes a fine vantage point for watching the birds and boats go by. (See plan below.) Design: Mel and Joanne O'Neil.

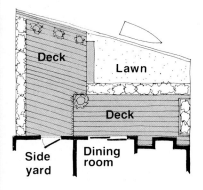

**39**

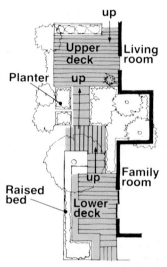

**Up-the-hill decks** *take advantage of a sloping yard to provide two outdoor activity areas. Lower deck, handy to family room and kitchen, is framed with a built-in bench and raised beds for annuals. Upper deck opens off living room. About midway on lower level, decking switches from 2 by 6s laid flat to 2 by 4s laid on edge. (See plan above.) Design: Herr/Smith Associates.*

# WITH NO LEVEL LAND, SPLIT-LEVEL DECKS

## Before the decks, these yards were too steep to use; now each has two outdoor activity areas

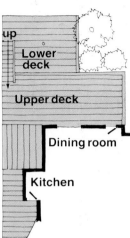

up

Lower deck

Upper deck

Dining room

Kitchen

**Two spacious outdoor rooms** were created when owners used decking lumber to level their steeply pitched back yard. Linked by a flight of garden stairs (see plan above), decks give adults an outdoor dining room (left) and children plenty of elbow room on lower-level game court (below). Design: Bo Tegelvik.

# THREE DECKS FOR A HILLSIDE HOME

## From entry, bedroom, and upstairs study, easy routes to outdoor rooms

**Spacious entry deck** was first of three solutions owners found when they remodeled their sloping garden to create outdoor living space. Now the first of three deck levels, the new entry replaces a small front porch. It projects 16 feet over garden slope, angles around a shade tree, and steps up to a mid-level deck (see plan at right). Design: Morris M. Skenderian.

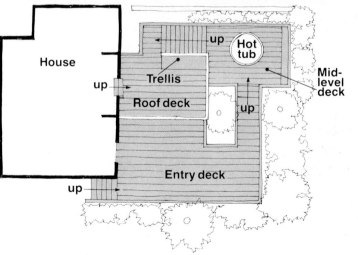

House

up

up — Trellis

Roof deck

up

Hot tub

Mid-level deck

up

Entry deck

up

**Mid-level deck,** *linked to entry deck by an engawalike walk, surrounds a sunken, solar-heated hot tub. Surrounded itself by high shrubs and a wall of blooming impatiens, this deck has a secluded feeling.*

**Rooftop aerie** *offers an expansive ocean view, yet has the feeling of a retreat, thanks to a high vertical screen. Designed to give privacy from neighbors' view, screen was built of 1 by 2s and 1 by 6s alternated in a sturdy redwood frame.*

**Lath canopy and privacy screen**
lend a feeling of seclusion to a small
redwood deck exposed to neighbor-
ing second-story windows. Deck,
raised 2 feet above grade to be level
with adjacent kitchen and study
(see plan below), offers two routes
into garden. Wide built-in bench
keeps need for additional outdoor
furniture to a minimum.
Design: Donald G. Boos.

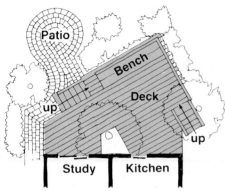

# MAKING THE MOST OF THE SQUEEZE-PLAY YARD

### It's surprising how livable a small yard can be

**With only inches to spare,** *owners stretched a low-level deck as near the lot line as possible when they remodeled their garden. Linked to a smaller platform by an angular step, deck has a fire ring made of fire-bricks, set on end and mortared. Design: Richard Carothers Associates.*

**Classic cedar deck** *(below) strikes a contemporary chord with bold painting hung along high shingled wall. Access to 14 by 18-foot deck is through new doors in dining room, or by way of garden steps built of 2 by 4s laid on edge. Design: Robert W. Chittock, Ben Ridgway.*

# DECK IDEAS FOR NARROW LOTS

## They changed levels to break up space

**Boldly designed garden bench** and screen became focal point when a narrow yard was remodeled to include a wood deck. Because it's situated near property line, bench makes yard seem deeper than its 10 feet. Steps on deck's far side (see plan below) lead to a concrete patio. Design: Robert Perron.

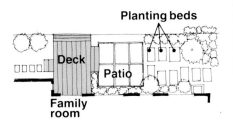

Planting beds
Deck
Patio
Family room

**Cantilevered** a little over a steep hillside, new deck and brick paving turned a 6-foot-wide concrete slab into a charming outdoor living area, accessible from four rooms in house (see plan below). Overhead trellis units can be adjusted or removed to control light. Design: Tom Silvers.

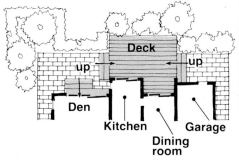

Deck
up
up
Den
Kitchen
Garage
Dining room

***You step up, then down*** to reach each of three redwood decks scattered the length of this wedge-shaped yard (see plan below). Change in levels created by wood bridges helps separate each outdoor living area and draws the eye above an otherwise flat plane. Cedar stepping pads in a rich carpet of Scotch moss (right) link decks to interior rooms. Garden stairs lead to upper terrace.
Design: Robert S. Rubel.

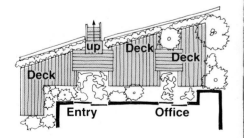

# GAINING SPACE: FOUR IDEAS FOR HILLSIDE SITES

## A deck can put a hill to work, opening space and views

**To make room** for an oceanfront sun deck (above), owners carved a 12-foot-wide ledge out of their steep back yard. New deck has a bench extending the length of brick retaining wall, plus tempered glass screens that let view in but keep wind out. Steps at right lead to upper terrace. Design: Richard E. Harrington.

**Handsome, arbor-sheltered deck** (left) replaced what at one time was nothing more than a steep bank with barely enough room for a narrow concrete walk. Supported by sturdy concrete posts, new deck extends slightly beyond a stone retaining wall (see sketch below). Decking was laid in a checkerboard pattern between boards stained to match arbor. Design: Eriksson, Peters & Thoms.

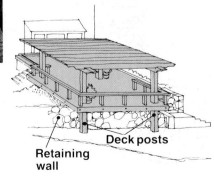

Deck posts

Retaining wall

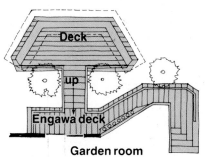

**Deck**

**up**

**Engawa deck**

**Garden room**

**To add level space** to their hillside site without sacrificing two stately cypress trees, owners built a bridge between trees and pushed deck away from house (see plan above). Lath arbor conceals wiring for outdoor lighting. Steps in foreground lead to a narrow engawa deck that wraps around garden room. Design: Donald G. Boos.

**S-curved deck,** built around a freeform swimming pool, follows pool contours and bends around a hillside oak. Sheltered by trees, deck offers poolside shade and almost 600 square feet of level living space. Design: Mary Gordon.

# STREAMLINED SUPPORTS FOR HIGH-LEVEL DECKS
### Two decks "float," the third is one-legged

**Floating above a sea of trees,** *handsome cantilevered deck is supported both by heavy laminated beams that extend from house, and by steel tension rods that reach from roof beams to deck. Tension rods help to tie deck's weight back to main structure. Design: James A. Jennings.*

**Sturdy timber crutches** *support a cantilevered gangway and deck that boldly projects over a slope. Timbers are joined with steel tie plates and anchored to house; this way, they transfer deck's weight back to foundation. Though 35 feet long, deck measures only 9 feet at its widest point. Design: Robert K. Overstreet.*

**Long-legged pedestal** *carries the weight of a roof-level deck raised 18 feet above grade to take full advantage of a view. Pedestal, built of four 4 by 4s, supports multiple beams that run beneath center of deck. Joists are braced on either side and anchored to house wall. Design: Carlton C. Kovell.*

# WOOD & WATER: DECK IDEAS FOR POOLS, TUBS, LAKEFRONT LOTS

**Two have first-row seats on the waterfront**

*Sun deck* built right at water's edge accommodates both boaters and bathers—dock doubles as diving platform. Adjacent is a small sandy beach that's protected from breeze by a concrete retaining wall (see garden plan below). Design: Chaffee-Zumwalt Associates.

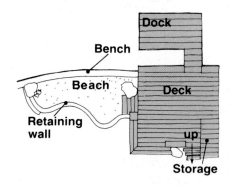

Dock
Bench
Beach
Deck
Retaining wall
up
Storage

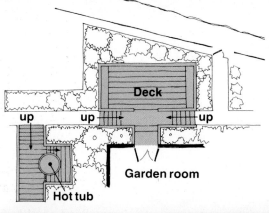

**Deck**

up        up        up

**Garden room**

**Hot tub**

**Shingle-sided cedar decks,** *one for entertaining (above), the other for hot-water soaking (above left), make double use of a waterfront setting (see garden plan at left). Designed to suit architecture of house, both decks have shingles painted to match house siding, railings painted to match house trim. Design: Bennett, Johnson, Slenes & Smith.*

**Poolside deck** *seems to float, thanks to rocks that are partially embedded in concrete to camouflage piers and footings. Judiciously arranged throughout garden are more rocks, adding variety to yard's linear look. Decking on both sides of pool is redwood, laid in a parallel pattern with alternating 2 by 2s and 2 by 6s. Design: Lang & Wood.*

# FREESTANDING DECKS THAT FIT POCKETS IN THE GARDEN

## They can change the way you live outdoors

**Little six-sided deck,** *tucked into the shade of two liquidambar trees, turned an unused garden corner into a favorite outdoor sitting spot. Nearby garden pool is fed by a recirculating waterfall. Design: Mary Gordon.*

**Gazebolike pavilion,** *12 feet square, is roomy enough for a small crowd, cozy enough for just one or two. Sheltered by a lath canopy, deck is surfaced with 2 by 6s laid in a checkerboard pattern. Built-in benches rest on supports bolted to vertical posts. Design: Tom Higley.*

**Rectangular redwood deck,** wedged into a berm in back yard, draws attention to garden and gives youngsters a compact play platform. Deck was surfaced with 2 by 2s and 2 by 6s laid in concentric squares over a diagonal joist system. Wood retaining wall supports built-in bench. Design: Lang & Wood.

**Shingle-roofed gazebo** (above) offers instant shade in a sunny, rock-studded garden. Measuring just 10 feet from edge to edge, the octagonal gazebo is sheltered from wind by a row of cedar, cypress, and pine trees. Design: Heinz Koenig.

**Shaded sculptured deck** (left) invites you into the garden for early morning coffee, evening conversation. Nestled in a cluster of evergreens, deck is just a step away from master bedroom and nearby patio. Design: C. A. and Elva Powell.

# STRIKING BLENDS OF DECKS & SETTINGS

### Three decks designed to suit the landscape

**Winding through a wooded setting,** cedar decks lead you over a dry creek, around several aspen trees, and up some steps to a private sitting area framed with built-in benches. Designed to follow property's natural contours, decks border a small bubbling stream. Design: Chaffee-Zumwalt Associates.

**Situated atop a rugged cliff,** naturally weathered deck captures a sweeping coastal view. Deck was generously sized to suit magnitude of landscape and proportions of cypress tree around which it was built. Two steps down from main deck, a smaller platform catches ocean mists. Design: Ted Richter & Bob Haller.

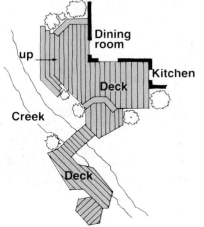

Dining room

up

Kitchen

Deck

Creek

Deck

***Tranquil garden feeling*** *is achieved with wood decking designed to bridge a small natural creek. On one side of creek, deck spacious enough for entertaining is accessible from dining room through two sets of French doors (above). On other side (right), deck meanders toward a sheltered glade just right for reading and other quiet pursuits. (See plan at left.) Design: John Herbst, Jr.*

# OUTDOOR ROOMS WITH AN INDOOR FEELING

## Ways to turn wood into garden rooms

**Elegant poolside teahouse** *is twice functional—first as a sheltered entertaining center, second as a storage unit for pool's support system. Nearby, a rock-floored stream and waterfall circulate water back to pool. Design: Kimio Kimura.*

**Japanese garden room** *(right) replaced an old concrete patio, providing owners with year-round indoor-outdoor living. On warm days, shojilike screens (above) slide aside and stack to let in fresh air. During cool weather, panels are closed and deck becomes a sunlit garden room. Overhead skylights have fabric shades that can be adjusted to let in more light. Design: Alan Oshima.*

**Grove of lanky cedar trees** *provides a dignified setting for a gazebo tailored to adult entertaining. Groups of cedar posts support built-in bench and roof, as well as overhead lighting fixtures concealed by horizontal wood strips. Design: Robert C. Slenes and Morton Safford James III for Bennett, Johnson, Slenes & Smith.*

**Glass-walled atrium,** *floored with redwood planks, gives three interior rooms a year-round garden view. Plants thrive in a climate that is controlled, in part, by a translucent skylight that opens and shuts electrically. Design: Siong and Lily Lim.*

**59**

# THEY TURNED ROOFS INTO ROOFTOP DECKS

## This way you can have a deck and your garden too

*Linked to the house* with a second-story bridge, converted garage roof (right) provides generous outdoor living space on a tight city lot. Decking and lattice rails are both hemlock, though lattice was painted to match trim of house (below right). Stairs lead to a shaded, ground-level courtyard (see garden plan below). Design: Ron Pimentel.

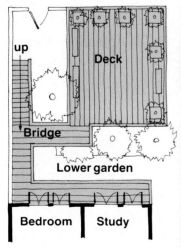

up

Deck

Bridge

Lower garden

Bedroom    Study

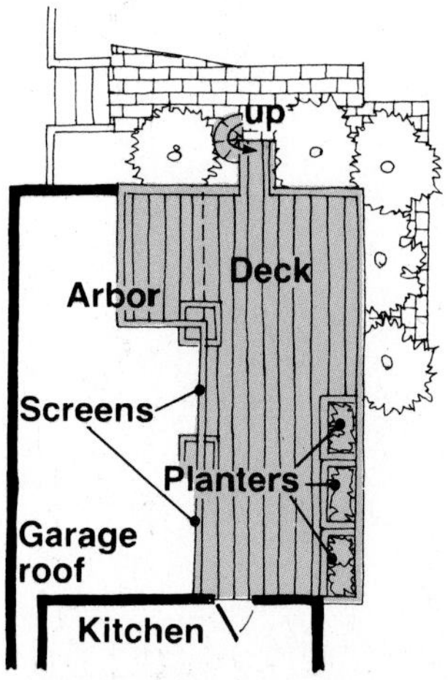
up
Deck
Arbor
Screens
Planters
Garage
roof
Kitchen

***You can choose*** *between sun and shade (below) when you step outdoors to a roof deck designed with both in mind. Main deck catches pleasant morning light; lath-covered alcove offers an intimate, shaded spot for reading and conversation. Accessible either through a door off kitchen (right) or up spiral stairs from garden, the deck is shielded from undeveloped roof area by cedar screens and planters (see garden plan at left). Design: Robert W. Chittock.*

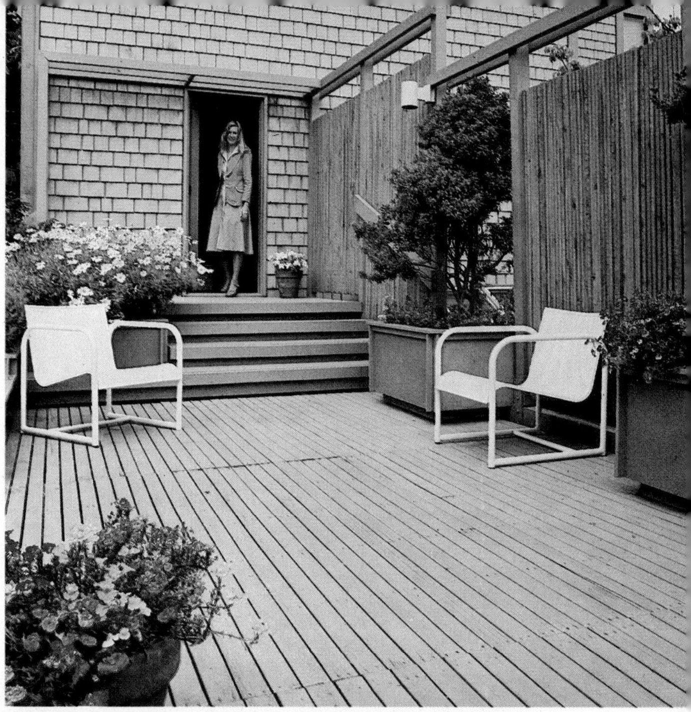

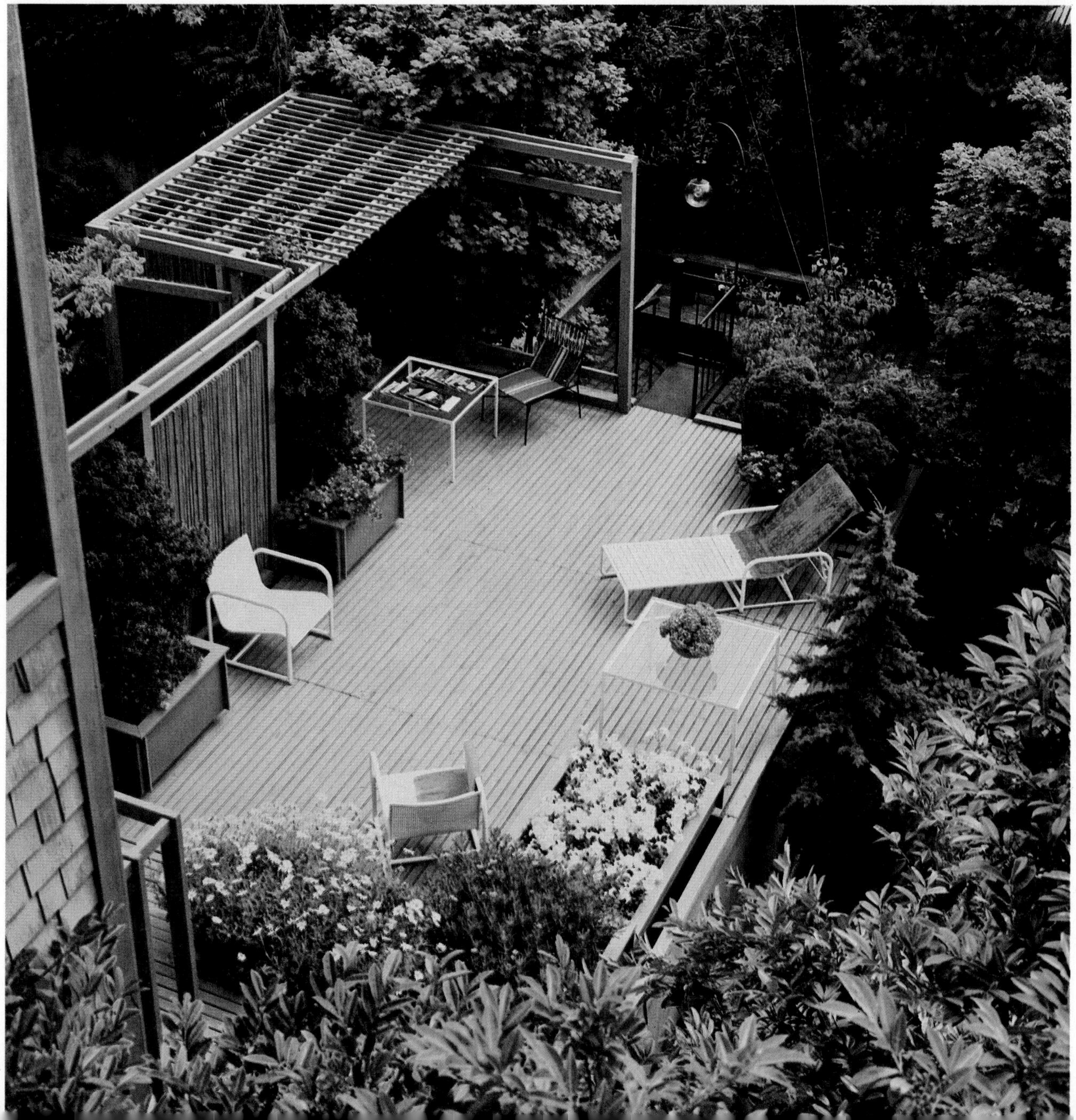

# A CLOSE-UP LOOK AT BENCHES & RAILINGS

## From a legion of options, seven suggestions

*Curve in railing,* created with flexible 1 by 4s and 1 by 6s, gives a contemporary feeling to a traditional setting. Posts are built of three 2 by 6s; one extends down deck's skirt to foundation. Design: Wallace K. Huntington.

*Steel tubes* make sturdy side railings for a high-level entry deck. Two-inch-diameter tubes were painted to match the house and slipped through holes drilled in fir posts. Design: Robert and Laura Migliori.

**Spaced 1 by 2s** make a comfortable, ventilated bench that won't collect water. Design: Herr/Smith Associates.

**Within a hinged bench,** handy garden storage center contains potting supplies and small tools. Bench surface is solid to keep rain out. Design: Ed Hoiland.

**Screens of tempered glass** installed between wooden posts block out wind but preserve view. (For another view of this deck, see page 48.) Design: Richard E. Harrington.

**Slant-backed bench** functions equally well as a sturdy side railing. Posts for railing are pairs of 2 by 12s bolted to deck's substructure; bench supports are bolted between posts. Design: John McInnis.

**Double-duty bench** was broadened at one end to create table space for alfresco meals. Covered with cushions, it's a sunbathing platform. Design: Harlow L. Williams, Jr.

# SEVEN WAYS OF CHANGING LEVELS
### Good-looking stairs . . .
### with the focus on function

*Like a stack of nesting boxes,* steps at right lead through a wooded garden from one deck level to the next. Mid-level platform is large enough to accommodate a bench. Design: Steve Burris.

*Steps on three sides* provide easy access to a five-sided pocket deck designed to make use of a sloping garden corner. The steps, simply built with redwood 2 by 6s, also provide extra seating for casual gatherings. Design: Mary Gordon.

**Forming herringbone patterns,** squares surfaced with a combination of 2 by 4s and 2 by 6s make an eye-catching link between ground level and deck. Design: John Bentley.

**Single center beam** supports uncomplicated garden stairs. Large bolts secure riser blocks. Design: Robert W. Champion.

**Irregular, "floating" steps** are supported by steel pipes set in concrete footings. Design: Robert M. Babcock.

**Angular tread,** like conventional ones, is framed with mitered boards, adding a custom touch to traditional garden steps. Design: Armstrong & Sharfman.

**Sturdy steps** can be built with either 2 by 2s or 2 by 4s set on edge, with spacers between. Design: Herr/Smith Associates.

# HOW TO ESTIMATE & ORDER MATERIALS

**You save time & money if you**

- **choose the right grades & types**
- **minimize waste wood**
- **order all you'll need at once**

Estimating and ordering materials for a deck is not complex, but the process is important. Done well, it saves money. Done carelessly, it can cost both time and money.

The trick in estimating is to pinpoint volumes or amounts of material, always with a slight margin for waste and error, so that you can make all purchases at once.

The most important aspect of ordering is specifying grades, qualities, and sizes (dimensions and lengths in lumber, diameters and lengths in bolts or screws, for example. Here, the goal is to find the most economical material that fits into your plan both as a matter of workability and appearance.

This may be subtler work than it sounds. As noted in the chapter on planning, there are many grades and species of wood suitable to building any one deck—each of them at a differing price from the rest. In addition, unless the deck measures an even number of feet in both length and width, the lengths chosen can affect the amount of waste. That is, for a deck requiring 15-foot joists, buying 16-footers may not be as cost efficient as buying all 10-footers.

Some lumberyards will take back unused materials, usually with a charge for handling. Even with this option, though, a sound estimate and purchase will save time and, possibly, extra delivery charges.

## Estimating building materials

Estimating is primarily a matter of measuring and counting the number of pieces necessary to complete your project. Ballpark estimates made early in your planning will help you to compare costs of different deck surface and substructure arrangements; a detailed estimate of the final plan provides a basis for ordering materials.

You are ready to prepare final estimates once you have completed the final scale drawings of your deck. If you are working with a contractor, he or she will probably arrange estimates (and orders) unless you make some other arrangement. If you are working with an architect, the architect will probably specify materials, but you may have the responsibility of listing and ordering them.

## Estimating deck surface lumber

Your finished scale drawing should tell you how long deck planks should be and how many are required to fill the surface area.

**Figuring board lengths.** To estimate the length of the lumber required for your project, use your scale drawing to measure how long decking must be to reach from one end to the other—in the direction perpendicular to the joists. Then round off the dimension to the next highest foot. Plan to order lumber in the rounded length or in increments that combine to produce it. Keep in mind that lumber is generally stocked in even lengths. If you need an 11-foot board, for example, plan a combination of 8 and 6-foot lumber that can be cut and butted together over a joist or beam (two 8-foot boards plus one halved 6-foot board produce two 11 footers). or 12-foot lumber that can be cut to size.

**Figuring quantity.** To estimate the number of boards you'll need, you can either measure to scale and count the number of pieces, or you can use the formula that follows.

The coverage formula tells you how many boards of a specific width will cover 1 foot of a deck's width. assuming a standard $\frac{3}{16}$-inch spacing between planks.

*Number of 2 by 4s laid flat =*
*3.3 × width covered*

*Number of 2 by 6s laid flat =*
*2.1 × width covered*

*Number of 2 by 2s, or edge-laid 2 by 3s or 2 by 4s = 7.1 × width covered*

In estimating, round your result to the next highest foot.

For example: For a deck 12 feet wide, using 2 by 4s: 12 × 3.3 = 39.6 boards, so you would order 40. If the deck were 12 feet 8 inches, you would use 13 × 3.3.

If the design blends different widths of dimension lumber in a repetitive pattern, you can estimate the coverage for each size lumber with the following formula:

*Number of pieces in a given size =*

$$\frac{\text{Coverage factor (3.3, 2.1, or 7.1)} \times \text{width covered}}{\text{Number of different widths used}}$$

For example, if a pattern combines 2 by 2s, 2 by 4s, and 2 by 6s, the divisor would be 3; if only 2 by 2s and 2 by 4s, the divisor would be 2, and so on. "Width covered" is the full deck dimension to the next highest foot.

If all deck planks are to be butted together, simply divide the deck's width in inches by the width of a single decking board. But keep in mind that a 2 by 6 measures 5½ inches wide, not 6. With all dimension lumber, actual dimensions differ from nominal dimensions (see chart on page 94).

## Estimating T&G lumber

An easy guideline for estimating tongue-and-groove coverage (whether you use it for subflooring or the deck surface) is this: subtract 1 inch from the nominal width of 1 by 6s. 2 by 6s, or narrower widths (not counting the tongue) or subtract 1¾ inches from wider standard widths.

For example, to find the width ten 1 by 4s will cover, first subtract 1 inch from the 4-inch dimension, then multiply the remainder (3) by 10. Ten 1 by 4s, fitted together, would cover a width of 30 inches.

## Estimating plywood

The only rules you need when figuring the coverage of plywood is that one pair of the panel edges should fall on joist centers (unless you are using the ⅞, 1, or 1⅛-inch interlocking panels), joints between panels should be staggered, and that the face grain of the panels should be perpendicular to the joists (or beams). With this in mind, sketch the standard 4 by 8-foot panels over the joist system you have planned and count them.

## Substructure members

No handy rules are available for estimating the amounts of materials you will need for the deck's substructure. Sizes and amounts differ with the slightest variations in substructure design. The best advice is to be sure that the design you have down on paper is as accurate as it can possibly be. Then make your estimates from the detailed drawings.

## Estimating concrete quantities

To determine concrete requirements, first roughly estimate the total volume to be filled (this is the amount of finished concrete required); then, unless you plan to purchase ready-mix concrete, estimate individual amounts of cement, sand, and gravel that together must total at least 1½ times the volume of in-place concrete after it has cured and dried.

**Figuring foundation volume.** You can approximate in cubic feet or cubic yards (27 cubic feet = 1 cubic yard) the total volume of footings and piers to be poured by multiplying the length by width by depth of each area and adding the results. Treat cylindrical, pyramidal, and irregularly shaped areas as though they were simple rectangular shapes; don't worry about their exact volumes. Avoid working in cumbersome cubic inches (1,728 cubic inches = 1 cubic foot) in this way: before multiplying, convert the lineal dimensions of the areas to approximate decimal equivalents of a foot based on 3 inches = .25 of a foot, 6 inches = .50, and 8 inches = .66. Then round out the total volume to the next highest cubic foot or cubic yard. For example, a total volume of 26.25 cubic feet becomes 27 cubic feet or 1 cubic yard.

**Determining ingredient amounts.** The basic formula for deck foundation concrete is one part cement to two parts sand and three parts gravel. To estimate the ingredients needed for concrete quantities other than those detailed below, adjust the amounts proportionately.

For 1 cubic yard of concrete, you will need five 94-pound sacks of cement, 12½ cubic feet of sand, 25 cubic feet of ¾-inch gravel, and 25 gallons of water.

To make 10 cubic feet of concrete, you will need 1⅘ sacks of cement, 4½ cubic feet of sand, 9 cubic feet of ¾-inch gravel, and 9 gallons of water.

The amount of water is based on 5 gallons per 94-pound sack of cement, and sand of average wetness. If your sand is very wet, use about 4¼ gallons per sack of cement. For barely damp sand, increase the water to 5½ gallons per sack.

For small quantities of concrete, you can purchase 90-pound sacks containing a dry mix of cement, sand, and gravel. Each sack will make about ⅔ cubic foot of finished concrete.

### Estimating hardware

Estimating metal connectors is simple. You merely count the numbers of posts, beams, and joists with which you will use connectors and tot up. Once a basic pattern is set, bolts and/or screws are similarly obvious.

Nails, on the other hand, are difficult to estimate. The best advice we can give is to assess your planned nailing pattern, count up the nails for a single unit, then multiply by the total units . . . and then add 10 percent. Better 15 percent. Having an oversupply doesn't directly lower costs, but it certainly avoids a midjob trip to the building supply store.

One other point about nails: For a weather-exposed deck, buy the best quality hot-dipped galvanized nails you can find. Any small saving from lesser quality nails will be more than offset by lost durability in the finished deck.

### Ordering materials

Procedures for purchasing materials in an orderly and economical manner should start with these two important steps:

1. Make a down-to-the-last-nail list of material needs taken from the completed and approved detailed deck plan drawing.

2. Plan carefully where on your property materials will be delivered. Keep in mind the distance to the construction site, damage to lawns and gardens, and "attractive nuisance" hazards to neighborhood children (you are legally liable if they are injured while playing on or with materials).

The next steps involve actually purchasing materials. By following the tips listed, you can get substantial savings on regular retail prices. For information on ordering concrete, see facing page.

### Cutting costs

The first basic rule of economy is to consolidate your purchasing. Order as many materials (lumber, nails, hardware, paint, and so forth) as possible at a single time from one supplier. *Avoid piece-by-piece material purchases, one of the most costly hazards of do-it-yourself construction.*

The second rule is to pick your major supplier on the basis of competitive bids from several retailers (provide each with an identical and complete list of material needs).

The third rule is to order materials in regularly available standard dimensions and in quantities 5 to 10 percent greater than your estimated needs.

In addition to these primary guides to economy, various other methods can help cut material costs in special situations.

### Ordering lumber

Order lumber only after you have accurately estimated the sizes and amounts you need—plus 5 to 10 percent extra. If your project is small you may be able to hand-pick lumber from your building supply center; if it is large, you may choose to order through a lumberyard. Those that specialize in selling lumber to contractors may offer a wider range of species and grades, as well as lower prices.

Lumber is sold either by the board foot or the lineal foot. When sold by the lineal foot, it is priced simply by its length. When sold by the board foot, however, lumber is priced according to the amount of wood in a piece of lumber equal to 1 foot long, 1 foot wide, and 1 inch thick.

To compute board feet in a piece of lumber, follow this formula: length (in feet) × nominal thickness (in inches) × width (in inches) ÷ 12. For example:

$12' \times 2'' \times 4'' \div 12 = 8$ board feet

$16' \times 4'' \times 4'' \div 12 = 21\frac{1}{3}$ board feet

**Contractor discounts.** If part of the construction is being done by a licensed contractor, he or she may arrange to purchase materials for you at a professional discount. If the entire deck is built under contract, these savings are normally included in the contractor's bid.

**Salvaged materials.** Many handsome decks have been built partially or wholly from materials salvaged from dismantled structures. Surplus shoring on heavy construction projects or driftwood found along seacoasts can also be used. Plywood, planks, timbers, poles, steel girders, and tile are typical salvage suitable for most deck building.

In some areas, wrecking companies specialize in the sale of such salvage. Contractors with dam, bridge, or large building projects nearing completion are also good sources; often you may have the materials free of charge if you'll haul them away.

*Warning:* Salvaged wood may require careful trimming to eliminate *all* weakening defects such as large bolt holes, toredo-worm borings, termite damage, or dry rot. Don't buy material with old nails or other fastenings still in the wood—they will damage saws and other cutting tools. Be sure to check local building codes before using salvaged materials.

### How to order concrete

To determine the best way of ordering ingredients and of preparing the concrete, first consider the size of your job. Whether you mix concrete on the site or have it delivered ready to pour as "transit-mix" (for 1 cubic yard or larger amounts), the cost of the materials will be about the same.

**Small decks.** For a few shallow footings under ready-made piers, the most convenient method is to use premixed, sacked-dry concrete. Mix it in a wheelbarrow, following the instructions on the bag. A 90-pound sack makes about ⅔ cubic foot of finished concrete.

**Medium-size decks.** To fill a concrete area of about 6 to 12 cubic feet most economically, buy the sand, gravel, and cement separately sacked in standard 100-pound bags. (In many areas, bulk deliveries of such small quantities involve an added delivery charge.)

**Large foundations.** Ordering sand and gravel by bulk is the least expensive method for large amounts of concrete to be mixed on the site. Minimum bulk orders without hauling penalties are usually 1 cubic yard or 1 ton of materials. Some suppliers will split this minimum order to include both sand and gravel in proportions to meet your requirements.

**Transit-mix concrete.** Ready-mix concrete delivered wet is particularly suited to *continuous* pours of 1 cubic yard (minimum order) or more. Interrupted pours usually involve time penalties for tying up the truck. Other major considerations in using this method are access of the truck to the site and the availability of enough helpers to allow for rapid handling of the deliveries.

## How to use the chart

The adjacent chart is meant only as a rough guide.

In general, the less experienced you are at building, the more entries your own chart should have—even to the point of separate lines for nails to be used in the substructure and in the deck surface.

Use your detailed drawing from the building permit application as a guide in setting up your chart.

## Sample Materials List

| | Size | Length | Quantity | Cost | Total Cost |
|---|---|---|---|---|---|
| **Foundation** | | | | | |
| **Concrete** | | | | | |
| **Sand** | | | | | |
| **Gravel** | | | | | |
| **Substructure** | | | | | |
| **Posts** | | | | | |
| | | | | | |
| **Beams** | | | | | |
| | | | | | |
| **Joists** | | | | | |
| **Ledger** | | | | | |
| **Bracing** | | | | | |
| | | | | | |
| **Framing** | | | | | |
| **Edging** | | | | | |
| **Surface Lumber** | | | | | |
| **Decking** | | | | | |
| | | | | | |
| | | | | | |
| **Misc. lumber** | | | | | |
| **Hardware** | | | | | |
| **Nails** | | | | | |
| **Screws** | | | | | |
| **Bolts** | | | | | |
| **Post attachments** | | | | | |
| **Metal connectors** | | | | | |
| **Flashing** | | | | | |
| **Misc.** | | | | | |
| **Finishes** | | | | | |
| **Preservatives** | | | | | |
| **Stains** | | | | | |
| **Paints** | | | | | |

# BUILDING YOUR DECK

**Step-by-step instructions for**

- digging & pouring footings
- erecting simple or built-up posts
- assembling the substructure
- laying the deck's surface

Once you've planned where to put your deck, drawn a detailed design, and ordered the materials, the moment of truth is upon you. If you will have professional assistance in building the deck, the next step is an easy one: simply let your help know that building can commence at any time. If, on the other hand, you will be doing the work, roll up your sleeves, assemble your tools, tuck this book under your arm, and head for the construction site.

The information given here covers the basic procedures that you should follow for common types of decks—geared mainly toward the low-level deck. For variations, see "Drawing a Workable Deck Design," pages 22–31. Some deck parts that have many design possibilities (such as benches, overheads, or railings) are not discussed in this chapter. Instead their basic construction details are given along with the design information in the design chapter. Wooden members will probably need to be treated with preservatives against rot or termites *before* construction. See the next chapter, "Protecting Your Investment," beginning on page 84.

## Site preparation

The first step toward deck construction is preparing the site. Three considerations are important: proper drainage beneath the deck, minor grading of the site, and effective weed control.

### Drainage

Keeping the ground from getting too soggy is a larger problem for the owner of a flat lot than for the person who dwells on a hillside. Though a deck can bridge low spots that would otherwise get too boggy for use, the area it spans must be firm enough to support the structure.

The commonest method of drying a wet spot is to dig a ditch sloping away toward better drainage— either a previously installed drain system or natural drainage. The ditch should be at least 1 foot deep, and it should drop at least 1 inch every 15 feet. Where water runoff is normal, lay 4-inch sewer tile fitted loosely together on the floor of the ditch. Add a strip of builder's paper over the top of each joint to keep dirt from sifting through the pipe, cover the tile with about 8 inches of 1½-inch drain rock, then fill the ditch with dirt to grade level. In areas of extremely heavy runoff, place a 1-inch layer of drain rock on the ditch floor before laying tile so water will have freer access to the bottom of the tile. Where runoff is slight, a ditch filled with drain rock alone will be sufficient.

### Typical drainage system

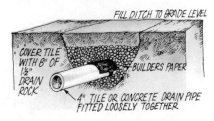

A dry well at the lowest point of a wet spot can solve drainage problems if soil conditions permit. Before planning such a well, check with a building inspector about restrictions. If you get approval, dig (with an earth auger or by hand) a straight-sided hole 24 to 36 inches in diameter down to good drainage. Fill it with large rocks. Drain rock 2 to 4 inches in diameter is excellent for this purpose. Be careful not to weaken the soil around the hole; otherwise enough can wash away over time to make the deck's footings insecure.

On a hillside site, drainage is more likely a matter of channeling surface runoff to minimize erosion. A successful technique for this is a concrete trough or spillway running downhill from a collection point. This system works in several situations: the commonest is catching surface water that weeps through holes in a retaining or foundation wall. If runoff is heavy, build the trough with a flare at the downhill end to slow water and spread it over an area planted to hold soil. An outfall of large rocks may be needed to prevent erosion in the extreme case.

### Grading

Not the happiest of tasks, grading is infrequently encountered in building decks. Even when it is necessary, the job is usually minor. Some lots may need a high spot or two knocked down to permit setting a deck at the house's indoor floor level or to keep deck parts from gaining too much altitude. An extremely bumpy site may need smoothing out. In any case, because soil needs careful repacking to support footings once it is loosened, the main concern is to avoid digging too deep. Careful grading can help solve drainage problems and can make measuring post heights easier.

### Weed control

No homeowner wants weeds sprouting between the boards of a new deck. Controls are several. Many low-level decks naturally prohibit new weed growth because they block light and air from nourishing the plants.

A serviceable and inexpensive nonchemical solution to ensure stopping weed growth is 6-mil or 10-mil polyethylene sheeting or 30-pound asphalt-felt builder's paper. The plastic or paper is spread on the cleared ground and covered with gravel where it is visible. Rocks or bricks, laid every few feet, keep the large sheets in place. Hold off on this job until just before you are ready to lay the decking across the substructure.

Any number of chemicals kill weeds; each should be approached with caution. Rapid developments in the chemical industry have produced a number of specialized weed control compounds. You can buy selective weed killers; volatile soil sterilants that kill all plant life, then leave the ground in 2 or 3 weeks; and permanent sterilants. Some of them—permanent Atrazine and Simazine are two—are highly toxic, and dangerous unless used properly. All of them can harm other plants when they are carried to the root zones by ground water. Unless you are familiar with the properties of these compounds and have used them, be careful. A friend who is an

experienced gardener or a nursery worker may be able to help you in choosing and applying one. Rock salt, which does not act as quickly as the commercial sterilants, poses similar problems.

## Placing footings & piers

Placing the foundation is the first actual construction step in deck building. As mentioned in the chapter on design, the foundation consists of two separate elements: footings and piers. Footings must always be poured on the spot; piers can be purchased preformed and set into place, or formed and poured along with their footings. Before considering how you will work with the concrete, figure the exact placement of each footing.

### Locating footings & piers

To locate accurately the footings and piers, first outline with string the edges of the proposed deck. Then, fasten a temporary ledger to the wall of the house (see page 72). The ledger will give you a stable, level surface from which to make your measurements. Build batterboards, placing them a foot or two outside the deck corners as shown below. Be sure to drive the batterboard stakes firmly into the ground; they must not move when you pull the strings taut. Level the tops of the batterboards with each other and with the top of the ledger; use a line level and mason's line or carpenter's level and straight 2 by 4 as shown below.

### How to level batterboards

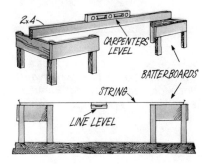

# The Building Sequence . . . from Start to Finish

Shown here in sequence are the major steps in building a simple low-level deck.

Sound planning of the phases of construction can save hours of waste motion. This page is not planned to be your sole reference for gathering the right tools and materials in the right place at the right time. Rather, it is meant to give an overall picture of the process and, at the same time, to serve as a guide to detailed information in this chapter.

It's a good idea to write out a schedule of jobs based on your own plan, especially if the deck has complications not shown here. (In particular, this page does not deal with extending posts upward to support railings or overheads; for this, see page 28.)

Throughout your work, use your level and tape twice as often as you think necessary. Remeasuring takes only a few seconds and frequently saves troublesome errors that must be undone and redone.

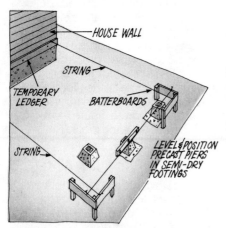

**1.** *Having established footing locations (page 71), dig footing holes, fill with wet concrete, and level precast piers into position (pages 73–74).*

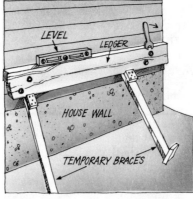

**2.** *Figure the deck height and prop the ledger where it should be to ensure that height; then fasten it into place. (Details pages 76–77.)*

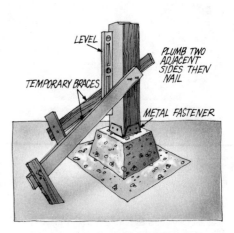

**3.** *Temporarily brace posts in place, measure, level with each other, and cut to proper height (page 77). Plumb before fastening to pier blocks.*

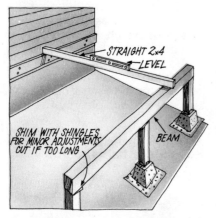

**4.** *Place beam across post tops and level it with ledger, or allow outward slope for drainage (page 78). After leveling across post tops, fasten.*

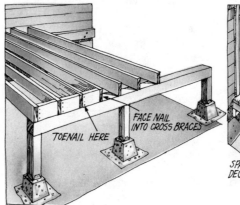

**5.** *Fasten joists in place (page 78) according to proper spacings (page 26). Use joist scraps to cross brace for rigidity (pages 79–80).*

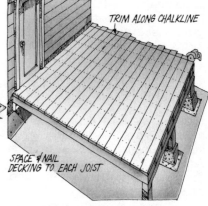

**6.** *Align decking across joists parallel to house wall and nail into place, spacing boards about 3/16 inch (page 81). Trim edges with power saw.*

**Squaring corners.** Tap an 8d or larger nail into the top of the ledger at one end, Point A. From A, measure 3 feet along the ledger and tap in another nail, Point B. Now stretch a string between A and the batter-board as shown. With a steel square make the string as perpendicular to the ledger as possible and fasten it to a nail, Point C. Measure 4 feet along the string from A and tie on a short piece of string to mark Point D. Measure the distance from B to D. If the corner at Point A is 90°, the distance will be exactly 5 feet. If it is not, adjust the position of C by moving the nail until it is. String stretches, so each time you move C, recheck the position of D and adjust if necessary. Then remeasure the distance from B to D. This system works in any multiples of 3-4-5—for instance, 6-8-10 or 9-12-15.

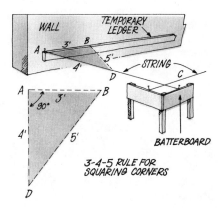

*3-4-5 RULE FOR SQUARING CORNERS*

With a 90° corner, secure the string at Point C and repeat the procedure for the remaining corners of the deck outline. When all strings are taut and secured, make a final check for level and measure diagonally from opposite corners (forming an X), making sure both measurements are the same. If they are the same, the layout is in proper alignment. If they are not, adjust until correct. Make a last check for proper deck surface outline dimensions.

**Using the string outline.** Use the information on pages 26–27 to figure the proper post spacings beneath beams or joists and thereby to figure the proper footing placement. If you wish to keep the footings and posts out of sight be-

neath a low-level deck, plan to set the footings back from the deck edges slightly.

If you are building a deck with quite a few interior footings, tie a line to parallel lines so it can slide and mark it with the footing location. Adjust the line to the proper distance from its parallel neighbor, then locate the footings under the marks, one row at a time. In all cases, the line should cover the outside edge of the footings so it won't be in your way.

## Setting footings & piers

To form footings, simply dig an appropriately sized hole in the

ground and fill it with freshly mixed concrete to within about 6 inches of ground level. If piers are being poured at the same time, place and level their wooden forms over the wet footing concrete. While the concrete is still plastic, insert any reinforcing bar necessary for linking footings and piers (follow the same procedure if you are forming concrete columns on footings).

If you use precast piers or masonry blocks for foundations, they should be soaked in water and positioned within 5 to 10 minutes after the footing is poured. If the footing hardens, an additional step is necessary to bond precast piers properly. You'll have to sluice off

## Four kinds of piers

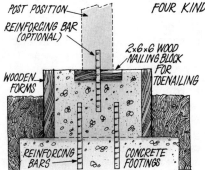

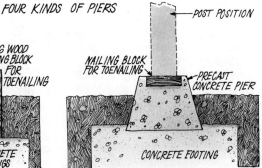

*FOUR KINDS OF PIERS*

**For formed pier,** concrete is poured into wooden form on top of semidry footing. Reinforcing bars add strength. Cap wet concrete pier with redwood nailer block or metal stirrup.

**Precast pier** is easy to work with. You simply set one into semidry footing, then level. Precast piers are purchased with nailer blocks set in place.

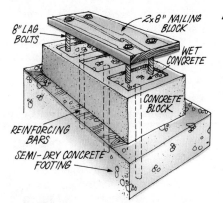

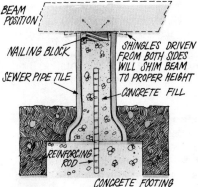

**Concrete blocks** can serve as piers if set into semidry footing. With reinforcing bar in position, fill core holes with concrete. Cap with nailer block anchored by legs.

**Sewer tile pipe** will make combination pier and post, but cannot be cut to adjust height. Nailer block and shims can be used to make fine adjustments beneath beam.

the top of the footings and bottom of the piers with water, then coat both surfaces with a creamy paste of cement and water (½ to 1 inch thick) to permit adjusting the piers to level.

Because of the core holes, concrete blocks are well suited to foundation construction. With reinforcing rods embedded in the semi-dry footings, seat the block, then fill the core with concrete. Last, rig a nailing block as shown on page 73. For low-level decks a few feet above ground, blocks can be stacked to eliminate posts entirely. Reinforcing rods must extend to the top.

## What to know about concrete

One of the first facts a builder should know is that "concrete" is not "cement." Concrete consists of cement, sand, gravel, and water. These ingredients are bonded together by chemical reaction between the water and the cement, a process that coats the particles of sand and gravel. Measuring the correct ratio of cement to water is the most critical part of making concrete.

The water should be clean and pure—good enough to drink. The sand must be clean river sand (the beach variety won't bond). Gravel should be a maximum of 1 inch in diameter and specially washed for concrete mixing.

If you object to the color of concrete, a number of dyes may be used in the mix (4 pounds per 100 pounds of cement). Burnt umber produces a dark and unobtrusive brown.

For information on estimating the quantities of concrete you will need, see page 67.

**Mixing concrete.** On-site mixing of small lots of concrete can be done in a wheelbarrow, using a shovel or hoe. Larger amounts are more easily handled with a rental half-bag mixer.

To mix by hand, spread two shovelfuls of sand and one of cement on the mixing surface. Using the shovel with a rolling motion, mix these ingredients until the color is even. Then add three shovelfuls of gravel and continue mixing dry for even color. Finally, scoop out a hole in the middle of the dry ingredients and add 3 quarts of water.

Work around the puddle with a shovel or a hoe, slowly rolling the dry ingredients into the water. Take particular care not to slop the water out of the wheelbarrow; escaping water may weaken the batch by carrying particles of cement with it.

If the batch is too stiff, add water a cup at a time and continue mixing until the proper consistency is reached. If it is too soupy, add small amounts of sand and gravel. Bear in mind that concrete at this stage of mixing changes consistency radically with the addition of even small amounts of ingredients.

To mix in a powered mixer, estimate the 1:2½:5 proportions of cement, sand, and gravel by shovelfuls. Add 2½ gallons of water per half-bag of cement. Tumble for 2 or 3 minutes. Pour into the wheelbarrow and dump into the form.

**Forming piers.** If scrap lumber is used for form material, it should be at least ½ inch thick. Old 3 to 5-gallon cans with tops and bottoms cut out also make good forms (pre-slit the sides and hold them in shape with wire to simplify removing them from the completed piers). Coat the insides of forms with clean engine oil to prevent concrete from sticking as it dries.

For thorough curing of the concrete, forms should be kept damp and left on for at least a week. If the curing piers are exposed to direct sun or hot, dry weather, cover them with newspapers, straw, or burlap sacks and keep moist.

Nailing blocks or attachment hardware should be embedded in the concrete immediately after the forms are filled. Use a carpenter's level to level them in place while the concrete is still plastic. If you are precasting piers separately from footings, be sure that the forms are poured on a level platform of scrap lumber (garage or patio floors also work well but first must be covered with building paper). Coat the inside of the forms with engine oil to prevent bonding of concrete.

## Concrete columns

Piers are sometimes extended upward to serve doubly as posts for decks (usually low-level decks). If the concrete posts are more than a foot high or if only a few are used, they should be reinforced with steel.

Neat cylindrical piers can be made with a manufactured form of fiber tubing, as mentioned in the chapter on materials. The tubing can be sawed to any desired length.

To make one, you first pour a concrete footing into a hole dug to requirements, then seat the fiber tube in the wet concrete. Check it with a level for vertical alignment (plumb), then seat the reinforcing rod (if required) deep into the footing. When the footing has partially hardened, fill the tube with standard 1:2½:5 concrete mix to the desired height. (See the section below on posts for techniques of determining the proper height.) Seat a nailer block in the top and check it for level. After the concrete has cured for a week or more, the tube can be stripped away.

You can form a similar post using ordinary sewer tile, seated with its joint end down in a footing. The tile comes in several usable diameters and in varying lengths. It is hard to work with if the site is not level since it does not yield readily to cutting. Square-sided concrete posts can be poured in wooden forms.

## Construction techniques

Before you begin working on the wooden substructure of the deck, you should know about techniques for building up large wooden structurals and splicing together joists and beams, as well as basic information on fastening with bolts and lag screws.

### Splicing & building up structurals

Rather than purchasing joists, beams, and posts in large one-piece timbers, various methods are used for splicing them together or building them up. Spliced or built-up structurals are usually easier to

## Splicing joists & beams

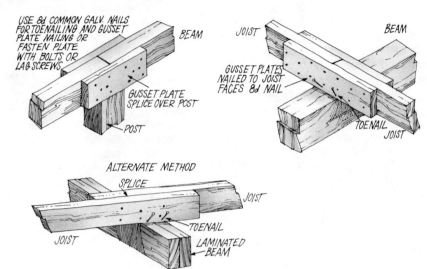

## Built-up structurals

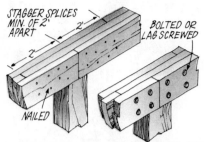

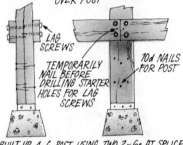

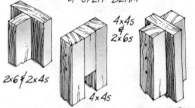

work with and less costly than the large-dimension lumber that you must otherwise special order (see "Ordering lumber," page 68). When properly designed and joined, spliced and built-up structurals are as strong as (and in some cases stronger than) single-piece members.

**Splicing joists & beams.** Typically joists and beams are spliced with board lumber "gusset plates" as illustrated; a splice must be supported by a beam or post. The ends of adjoining joists or beams are butted together over a supporting beam or post. Then two pieces of 1-inch-thick lumber of the same width as the joists or beam and about 18 inches long are nailed (with 8d common galvanized nails) on both sides of the splice. Be sure each end bears a full inch on the supporting member. If several spliced joists are needed, plan to stagger the splices over different beams to avoid weakening the substructure. Metal splice plates are available from building supply dealers.

Another splicing method for joists that breaks the uniformity of joist spacings but can be used in certain situations is simply to overlap them at the ends supported by beams as illustrated. If more than one splice is needed on a full joist length, over-

lapped sides should be alternated. Nail both faces of each splice with six 8d or 10d common galvanized nails. This type of splicing adds lateral stability to the joist system and may eliminate bracing (see pages 78–79).

**Building up beams & posts.** You can make large beams and posts by building up (nailing or bolting together) pieces of standard-width dimension lumber. Remember, though, that a built-up beam or post will not be as strong as a one-piece member of the same nominal size— a beam made of two 2 by 6s will be only 3 inches thick, compared to the 3½-inch thickness of a 4 by 6. Basically the same methods may be used for both beams and posts. Fastening details are illustrated above. Any variations you work out should follow the general rules given.

Related to building up timbers is the information on extending deck posts for railings and other above-deck structures that is given in the chapter on design under "Railings, benches, screens & overheads," page 28.

## Fastening with bolts & lag screws

The most rigid joints are held by bolts or lag screws. These heavy-

duty fasteners are recommended for any connections where strength is particularly important (beam-to-post, ledger-to-house, railing post-to-substructure, and so forth).

Two equally satisfactory types of bolts may be used: "carriage" or "machine" bolts (page 76). Standard diameters for deck use are in 1/16-inch increments from 1/4 inch to 3/4 inches; useful lengths are 3 to 12 inches. Bolts should be approximately 1 inch longer than the thickness of the combined pieces to accommodate washers and nuts. Plan to predrill bolt holes using a drill of the same diameter as the bolt's. Use washers under all nuts, and under heads of machine bolts only; carriage bolt heads bite into the wood, keeping the bolt from turning as you tighten the nut.

## Ways to bolt

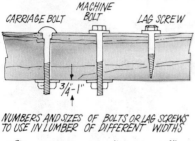

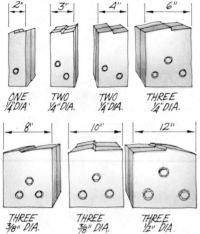

NUMBERS AND SIZES OF BOLTS OR LAG SCREWS TO USE IN LUMBER OF DIFFERENT WIDTHS

2"
ONE ¼" DIA.

3"
TWO ¼" DIA.

4"
TWO ¼" DIA.

6"
THREE ¼" DIA.

8"
THREE ⅜" DIA.

10"
THREE ⅜" DIA.

12"
THREE ½" DIA.

Lag screws are substitutes for bolts and come in equivalent sizes. They are particularly useful for tight spots where you can reach only one side of the connection with a wrench. Plan to predrill lead holes about two-thirds the length of the lag screws, using a drill ⅛ inch smaller than the lag screw shank. Use a washer under the head of each lag screw.

In softwoods, several small-diameter bolts or lag screws may be used at a connection instead of fewer large-diameter bolts. The number and size depend on the width of the lumber being joined. The most probable combinations are shown in the sketch above.

## Fastening ledger to house wall

Decks are connected to house walls by horizontal ledgers fastened through the house's exterior wall directly to interior floor framing or masonry foundation. Ledgers,

usually 2 by 4s or 2 by 6s, then support the ends of decking, joists, or beams. They are adequate only for relatively small decks; for high-level or large decks, use a 2 by 10-inch or wider ledger.

To avoid decay, the ledger must either be flashed or set out from the house wall by spacer blocks.

Joists may connect with a ledger in any of the ways used for joining joists to beams (see page 75). In some cases, decking rests directly on the ledger. Decking always should fit tight against the wall; flashing must extend as high as the top surface of the decking.

To make a firm deck-to-house attachment, use bolts or lag screws to connect the ledger to the header of the interior floor framing or to the masonry foundation wall (you'll need expansion anchors for the latter). If possible, avoid fastening the ledger to wall studs.

You can easily locate headers hidden behind an exterior wall by using architectural house plans. If your house has an unfinished room or basement adjacent to the deck site, you can probably see the headers from inside. If neither of these methods is possible, try another approach at the building

## Locating ledgers

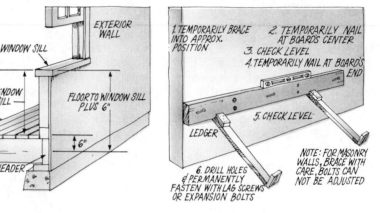

## Fastening ledgers

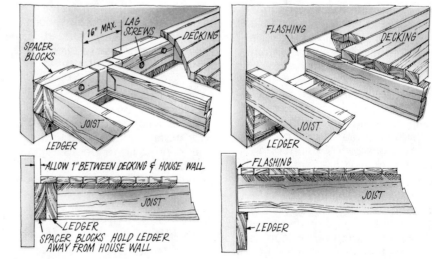

site: headers, usually 2 by 10s, generally have about 1½ inches of flooring and subflooring on top of them, so a satisfactory centerline for aiming fasteners into the headers is about 6 inches below the interior floor level. Use a window sill to find the measurements as shown in the sketch on the opposite page.

For fastening to solid concrete foundations, plan to use expansion bolts or lag screws in expansion shields. These fasteners should be at least 2 inches longer than the thickness of the ledger, spaced at a maximum of 2-foot intervals. For a concrete block foundation, place at least one fastener at the center of each block.

Here is the proper sequence of steps to follow: First, brace the ledger against the house wall at the desired height. For wooden walls, temporarily nail once at the board's approximate center, level the board with a carpenter's level, and temporarily nail both ends. Recheck for level. If you are working with stucco or masonry house walls, use makeshift braces for support. Drill lag screw holes through the ledger into the house's floor frame header or, for masonry, mark expansion shield holes on the wall and then drill, using a masonry bit. Bolt or lag screw the ledger in place. Remove braces, if any, and recheck level. If severely off level, remove the bolts or lags and begin again, first plugging and sealing the unused holes in the wall.

**Flashing.** Ledgers fastened directly to a house wall must be covered with galvanized metal flashing.

Once the ledger is in place, measure up the thickness of the decking plus joists (or just the thickness of the decking if it is to rest directly on the ledger). Add the width of the ledger plus an extra inch. Crimp the sheet metal to fit as shown. (To make a form for crimping, clamp two 2 by 4s together; use a hammer to pound a sharp edge at each fold.) Fit the flashing in place, bead the top edge with mastic, and nail it in place with galvanized nails long enough to penetrate at least 1 inch into wall studs or other structural members. If the house is finished

with shingles or lapped siding, the top edge of the flashing should be slipped up under the bottom edges as far as possible. Daub the nail heads with mastic.

**Ledger with spacer blocks.** A somewhat less decay-resistant alternative to flashing is a ledger set out from the house wall by spacer blocks. The blocks are spaced at the intervals determined by the bolts or lag screws. The blocks should be approximately 6 inches wide.

## Erecting posts

If your deck will be at a very low level, its "posts" may simply be short spacer blocks for keeping beams level over piers. If, on the other hand, one or more posts will stand very tall, you will have to measure and cut them at the correct height and find a means for propping them into place for fastening.

If you are building a deck that will require railings, benches, overheads, and so forth, consider the extended-post assemblies discussed and illustrated on page 28.

### Measuring for height

Accurately measuring post heights is an all-important phase in building a deck; you cannot achieve a stable horizontal substructure without precise measurements and fittings. For house-attached decks, first work on the posts farthest from the house. For freestanding decks, begin

working on the posts that support opposite edges and corners of the deck, then do any intermediate posts. The measuring operations for posts of freestanding decks are different from those for house-attached decks in only one respect: with the attached deck, you have already defined the height of the deck at the ledger line along the wall. For freestanding decks, erect a post at the approximate height (slightly taller), mark the height you wish on that post, and work from it as you would from a ledger on a house wall. The construction examples given here are for house-attached decks with both beams and joists; if yours will be different, adjust the directions accordingly. You decide which method will work best for you, considering the slope of your land, the post's length, and other factors.

If you think the deck should slope slightly for drainage of its surface, tilt your otherwise level marks downward (away from the house) about 1 inch for every 10 feet. Be sure to brush preservative on the raw ends of any posts that you trim.

**Measuring method 1.** Cut two posts 6 to 12 inches longer than estimated finish lengths. Bracing them firmly in place, plumb them, using a carpenter's level (check two adjacent sides of each post). Once they are plumb, permanently fasten posts to nailing blocks or post anchors on piers (page 73). Use a line level on a string secured to the top of the ledger to establish a mark on the post level with the ledger's

### Two ways to measure posts

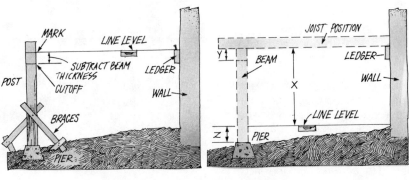

top. From that mark, subtract the thickness (actual, not nominal dimension) of the beam and make a new mark. This is your cutting line. Using a stepladder if necessary, cut the post in place.

If you don't have a line level for the measuring process, use a carpenter's level and a straight piece of lumber of adequate length.

**Measuring method 2.** This method is the same as method 1 except for one procedure: rather than fastening the post permanently in place, brace it temporarily and take it down to cut it.

You can cut other posts to the same length if the footings are exactly level with each other. Otherwise, it is best to repeat the process for each post.

**Measuring method 3.** On steeply sloping lots, you may find this method easier but not quite as accurate as those preceding.

Having established the ledger line as described above, measure from it down to the ground line of the house, establishing a base line at the latter point. From the base, run a line level out to a footing (or out over a row of them). Level the line and measure the distance that each footing comes above or below the house line.

To compute the post length, take the distance between the base line and the ledger line (x). Subtract the beam thickness (y) and add the difference between the footing and the base line (z). Check each post individually.

### Raising posts

Although it won't take a herculean effort to raise a post that is only 1 or 2 feet long, if the post is 8 to 12 feet long, you may need a helper. Drive stakes into the ground and nail a brace made from a 1 by 2 or 1 by 3 to each stake (with one nail—so they can pivot) before moving the post into position. Be sure to place these stakes where you won't have any trouble nailing the scrap pieces to the post sides once the post is in place. The stakes should be positioned far enough from the end of the post—and the braces should be

long enough—to reach halfway up the post at a 45° angle.

For long, heavy posts, place the bottom end near or on the footing and lift from the other end. Once it is vertical and squarely seated on the pier's nailing block or in its stirrup, check the post for plumb and correct if needed, using a carpenter's level on adjacent sides or a plumb bob mounted on a corner. Finish nailing the braces to the post. If you are permanently positioning it, connect it to the pier by nailing or lag screwing it to its stirrup or toenailing it to the nailing block.

### Seating beams

Hoisting a good-sized beam atop a post that stands to your shoulder or higher is equivalent to a good half-hour's calisthenics workout. If you have access to a block and tackle and know how to use it, do so. Otherwise, call in your sturdiest neighbor and follow this method:

Nail a pair of wooden cleats to the supporting posts' tops, forming a cradle on each (below). Drag the beam into rough position alongside the posts and slip a short length of 2 by 4 under one end of the beam. Using this to lift from both sides, raise that end of the beam and maneuver it into the cradle. Tie it down with a short length of rope so it won't slide off the post when you lift the other end. After a brief rest, attack the other end in the same way. Shim short posts up to proper height by

### Seating & fastening beams

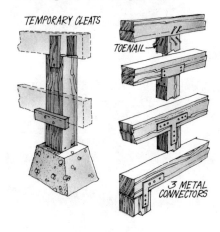

TEMPORARY CLEATS

TOENAIL

TOENAIL

3 METAL CONNECTORS

driving shingles between the post and beam.

You can fasten the beam into place using any of several methods. The simplest is toenailing with 20d common galvanized nails. For a stronger joint, leave the cleats on the post's top and nail them to the beam as well. Metal connectors are also available.

### Installing joists

Here are two common methods for securing joists: set each joist on top of a beam or ledger and toenail it in place; or set each joist into metal joist hangers nailed to ledger and beams.

Set and fasten both outside joists on opposite deck edges first; square each of them perpendicular to the house or perpendicular to beams, using the 3-4-5 method (page 73) or a large steel carpenter's square. Working from either outside joist, set, space, and fasten other joists. The last joist in place may be set closer to the deck's outside joist than the joist spacing specified in the design chapter. If you plan to use solid plate cross bracing (see below), precut braces, installing them as joists are placed. Mitered cross braces are more easily nailed after all joists are secured to beams.

### Ways to secure joists

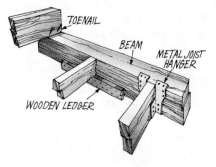

TOENAIL

BEAM

METAL JOIST HANGER

WOODEN LEDGER

### Cross bracing joists & posts

Long joist spans and wide spacing may allow joists to twist or buckle if they are not cross braced. The width of the joists is also a consideration; 2 by 12 and 2 by 8 joists require more cross bracing or "bridging" than 2 by 6s. Three common methods of cross bracing are illustrated. If the braces are not fitted and fastened to the joists, they serve no useful purpose. For this reason, spacers are preferred.

## How to brace joists

Those who would rather not make their own bridging can purchase manufactured metal cross braces. These cross braces, available in several varieties, are easily fastened to joists and save the tedious labor of cutting cross braces from wood. As is apparent in the illustrations, rectangular cross braces are easier to cut than the X type bridging. The rectangular type may also serve as backing for fastening down decking materials.

If joist spans are under 8 feet, headers nailed across joist ends are adequate. Longer spans need bridging or spacers every 8 feet

and at least two rows for spans over 12 feet.

Cross bracing between deck posts shorter than 12 feet (also see "Deck loads & heights," page 27) is recommended in several situations: for freestanding decks higher than 5 feet above ground; for decks (regardless of height) projecting farther than 20 feet from the house or more than twice the attached side's length; and for decks exposed to high winds or heavy loads.

Normally at heights of less than 12 feet, only outside posts on un-

attached sides of the substructure need cross bracing. Use 2 by 4s for bracing across distances less than 8 feet, 2 by 6s for greater distances. Plan to bolt or lag screw cross braces to posts. Various cross bracing methods are shown above.

For tall posts, mark individual cross braces in position and cut them on the ground. After treating braces with preservative, temporarily nail them in place, drill pilot holes for bolts or lag screws, squirt holes with preservative, and permanently fasten with bolts or lag screws.

## How to brace posts

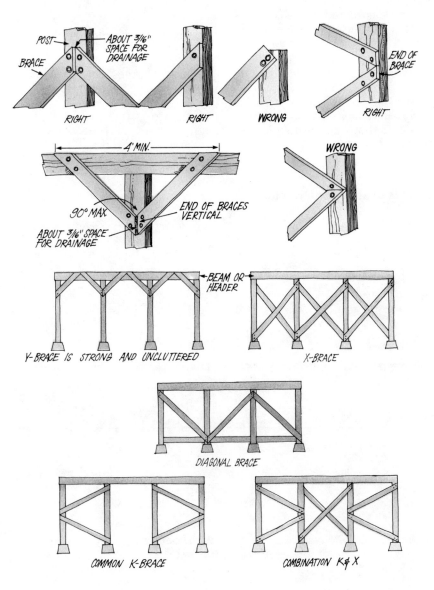

## Securing railing, bench, overhead, & screen supports

All supports that must be bolted or lag screwed to the substructure should be secured before decking is laid. Ways of bolting and interlocking these members to the substructure are given in the chapter on design, beginning on page 28. Treat the lumber with preservative (including bolt holes); prime it if you plan to paint it; and fasten it in place as shown in that section.

## Adding stairs or ramps

Because they must be tied into the substructure, the procedure of adding stairs or ramps is easiest if done before the surface decking is added. For design considerations, see page 30, "Steps, ramps & multilevels."

Sketches of two of the commonest methods for building a flight of wooden stairs are shown below. Stringers should be cut from 2 by 10s or 12s after they are worked out on paper. Treat them with a preservative before installation. Treat the treads, too.

Three 2 by 4s spaced ¼ inch apart make a tread of 11 inches; two 2 by 6s with ¼-inch spacing offer an 11¼-inch tread. You can visually tie the steps to the deck if you use the same material for the treads as for the decking.

If the stair or ramp is more than 4 feet wide, add a third stringer down the center. For extremely wide steps, plan a stringer every 4 feet. (These calculations presume 2-inch-thick lumber for treads.)

For a single flight of steps, secure tops of stringers to a beam or joist as shown below. Anchor lower ends of stair or ramp stringers as shown.

## Laying the decking

After selecting one of the surface patterns in the section on design, prepare the decking lumber by treating it with a preservative and (if you plan to paint it) a primer. If painting, make sure the preservative and the paint are compatible. Lay, square, and fasten the two outside pieces of decking at opposite edges of the deck. If the decking does not reach the full length of the deck, be sure to butt join the pieces directly over a joist (unless you are using tongue-and-groove). Stagger joints so that no two line up consecutively over one joist. If the appearance of the lumber permits, put boards bark side up to minimize checking and cupping. The bark side is the outer side of the growth rings, or the convex side. Lay out the rest of the decking on the joists in the surfacing pattern that you have selected and start spacing and fastening the decking in place from either edge.

**Spacing.** An important element, spacing can be accurately and uniformly accomplished by means of spacers. Perhaps the handiest is a 16d nail. Push the tip into the bearing surface snug against the board already secured. Shove the next board against the nail until it is held firmly, then secure that board. Yank the spacing nail and go on to the next bearing. If you wish different spacing, use a suitable nail or cut a

## Details of stair construction

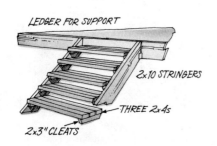

LEDGER FOR SUPPORT
2x10 STRINGERS
THREE 2x4s
2x3" CLEATS

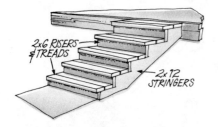

2x6 RISERS & TREADS
2x12 STRINGERS

**Stairs secured with cleats** are much simpler to build than those with treads cut into stringers.

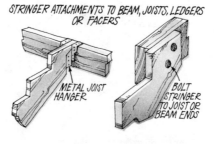

STRINGER ATTACHMENTS TO BEAM, JOISTS, LEDGERS OR FACERS
METAL JOIST HANGER
BOLT STRINGER TO JOIST OR BEAM ENDS

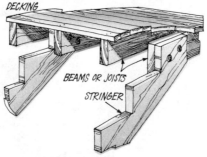

DECKING
BEAMS OR JOISTS
STRINGER

**With bolted stringer,** first tread is below deck; with joist hangers, first tread must be level with deck.

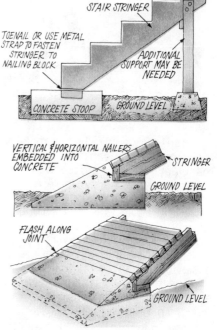

STAIR STRINGER
TOENAIL OR USE METAL STRAP TO FASTEN STRINGER TO NAILING BLOCK
ADDITIONAL SUPPORT MAY BE NEEDED
CONCRETE STOOP
GROUND LEVEL

VERTICAL & HORIZONTAL NAILERS EMBEDDED INTO CONCRETE
STRINGER
GROUND LEVEL

FLASH ALONG JOINT
GROUND LEVEL

**Bottom ends** of stringers must be anchored in a footing; ramps must have specially formed footings.

spacer from wood and use it in the same way. Make any spacing adjustments by slightly increasing or decreasing the distance between several pieces to avoid having to make a large adjustment on the last one. Spacing should never exceed ¼ inch. With narrow spacings, small objects won't slip through so easily, and high-heeled shoes won't be gripped by the cracks. Spacing is desirable as an aid to drainage and ventilation and should not be eliminated entirely without proper consideration.

## Laying decking

LEAVE ³⁄₁₆" SPACE BETWEEN DECKING ENDS

LUMBER BARK SIDE UP TO PREVENT CUPPING

**Nailing.** The quickest and least expensive way to fasten wooden decking or subflooring to joists or beams is, of course, nailing. Ring shank nails or other nails with threaded shanks are best; smooth-shanked nails tend to rise from decking as the wood's moisture content changes. Nails should be "hot-dipped galvanized." If aluminum or stainless steel nails are available, use them with redwood, cedar, or cypress to prevent discoloration of the wood. Do not use copper or poor quality galvanized nails. Nails should be long enough to penetrate the joists by at least the thickness of the decking.

Nail decking boards at every support point (joist or beam).

Your job will look neater and more professional if you keep nails in

a straight line, as in the patterns shown below. If you suspect that

### Nailing dimension lumber

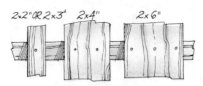

2x2" OR 2x3"   2x4"   2x6"

your decking is slightly green, you may wish to use only one nail at each bearing point when you first secure the decking, staggering them from side to side along the length of the board. The staggered nails will allow shrinkage during drying, but will not permit cupping. When the wood is cured, go back and complete the nailing.

A carpenter's trick to prevent splitting boards is to blunt the tip of each nail with a light tap of the hammer. To prevent splitting at the ends of boards, it may be necessary to drill pilot holes ¾ the diameter of the nail shanks.

For maximum holding power, drive nails perpendicular to the surface of the board, except when you're securing an end that will have another board butted against it. In this case, drive nails at 45° angles through the board and into the supporting member.

If you're installing plywood decking, it also should be nailed at each bearing surface, as shown in the sketch. To prevent bowing, nail two adjacent sides, starting from a corner (preferably a corner that butts against other sheets). If laminating two thicknesses, be sure to nail the underneath sheet in a consistent pattern that will allow you to nail the top sheets without having to guess where their nails must go to avoid the ones below.

### Nailing plywood

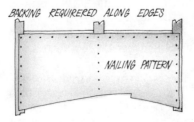

BACKING REQUIRERED ALONG EDGES

NAILING PATTERN

Tongue-and-groove or shiplap is blind-nailed, as shown in the sketches below. Blind-nailing minimizes

### Blind nailing

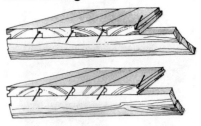

buckling due to swelling and shrinking with moisture changes. Also, nails cannot work up.

With any type of wood, it is useful to keep a small container of sealer or water repellent handy to splash on hammer dents; the sealer causes bruised wood to swell back to its normal shape.

The quantity of nails you'll need will depend on the decking width and joist spacings. As an example, 100 square feet of deck made with 2 x 6s on joists spaced 16 inches apart would require about 18 pounds of 20d common nails.

Owners of decks—especially low-level ones—that cover water or electrical lines may find it useful to secure three or more boards with screws to allow access for repairs.

If you do use screws, choose flat-head types long enough for 2/3 of the screw to penetrate the support member. With the boards in place, drill pilot holes through the decking and into the support members. (To assure alignment, push a nail into a pilot hole at each end before drilling the rest.) Pilot holes should be two sizes smaller in diameter than the screw size. Remove the boards and extend the pilot holes in the supports to half the depth the screws will penetrate.

Then, to make driving screws easier, drill the decking to accommodate the screws' shanks. Finish by countersinking so heads will recess into the deck.

**Cutting.** One tool that you should not be without when laying the decking is a portable circular saw. By using one of these, you can save

## How to fit decking around posts

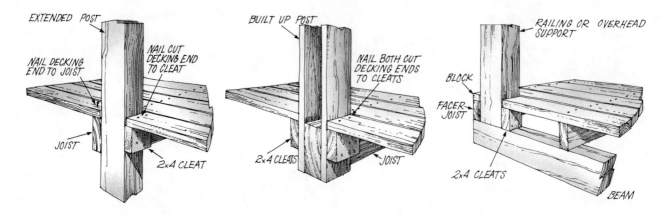

agonizing hours when cutting the boards to length. And if you've developed a bit of skill with the saw, you can trim off the deck's edges as squarely as any master carpenter. How? By cutting the decking after it has been laid.

Let decking boards run at least an inch past the edge lines of the deck; then when you finish nailing them all down, snap a chalk line carefully along the edges and saw along the line. Skilled hands can saw freehand along a chalk line. For those less experienced, a length of wood tacked to the deck can guide the saw.

**Special fitting problems.** Because posts for railings and similar structures must attach to substructure members, you may encounter problems when surfacing around them. Cutting individual pieces to fit presents no special problems. But being sure that those individual pieces are supported under both ends may create some extra work—joists and beams won't always be there for backing the boards. In these cases, you will have to install sturdy blocking between the nearby joists and beams. Some typical solutions are shown in the illustrations above.

## Trap doors for decks

Doors cut into decks can serve several functions. Among other useful ideas turned up during research for this book are these:

• In heavy snow country, a series of doors can be cut into the deck just outside sliding doors and windows that reach to floor level. In snowy weather, the trap doors are propped against window posts, as shown in the sketch. Snow cannot build up against the glass, even when heavy masses slide off the roof.

• A gardener stores hoses and other supplies in wells beneath the deck surface.

• A child's play deck uses a door atop a benchlike change of level as a storage bin for toys.

In all cases, the construction is similar, and simple.

The decking itself is cut so each end rests on a joist or beam. (The ends should reach half the width of a 2-inch supporting member; at least 1 inch should bear on a 4-inch support.)

On the underside of the door, a 2 by 4 or 2 by 2 strip should parallel each supporting member and fit snug against it to keep the door securely seated. To keep the surface uncluttered, these strips can be nailed from the underside with nails that penetrate 2/3 the thickness of the decking.

For extra support on a large door, strap metal can be secured on a diagonal.

Doors can be set in place for lifting out, or they can be hinged. If you opt for hinges, use leaf types, as shown in the sketch. It is useful to

drill a hole or to install a recessed ring to give a finger pull.

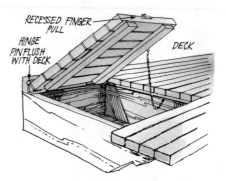

## Changeable decks

Most small decks—even such miniatures as engawas or poolside sun benches—call for conventional construction techniques from top to foundation. They are meant to be both permanent and durable.

However, reasons exist for building decks that are neither permanently fixed in place nor durable.

For one example, the family with children may wish a deck to serve as a play yard for a time, and then to grow up with the youngsters. The sandbox-and-bench shown on this page is an example of a feature that can either be removed or converted to use as a planter—in the same or a different location.

The sandbox or an even simpler variation also might be placed on a paved area.

For another example, a family facing the prospect of a job transfer or some other move may wish to install decking that can be carted along, or dismantled, but which in any case need not be imposed on the next owner or renter of the property.

The parquetlike modules also shown here are a simple, relatively inexpensive solution. They can be placed on rooftops, on paved areas, even on bricks or blocks in the garden so that spaces between can act as planters . . . and the units can be rearranged over and over to suit changing whims.

For such impermanent structures, the key is in building a framework that does not require foundations. Almost certainly this will impose limits on where such decking may be placed; codes will forbid it abutting the house or other code-protected structures.

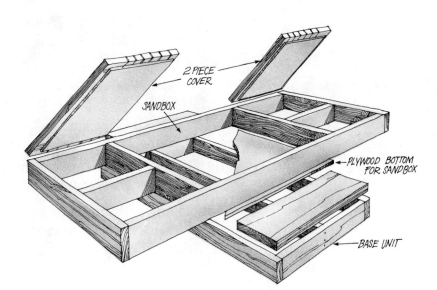

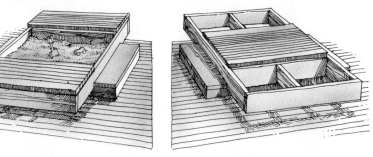

**Deck-top sandbox** *has base unit between it and deck to keep moisture from collecting. With varying number of cover sections, upper unit could serve as a sun bench, with or without an open end section for plants.*

**Modular boxes** *can be made in varying shapes and heights to produce an ever redesignable deck. Construction is simple, though larger units might require some crossbracing to eliminate excess flexibility. If used on bare earth, units should be made from pressure-treated wood.*

# PROTECTING YOUR INVESTMENT

## Choosing finishes & preservatives to give your deck

- ability to withstand decay
- resistance to weathering
- a finished appearance

Sooner or later, wood's natural enemies—decay-causing organisms, insects, and weather—will attack any wooden deck. However, treating a deck with preservatives and/or finishes can add years to its useful life. Even heart-grade redwood and cedar, disease resistant as they are, benefit from treatment more than enough to repay the cost.

Preservatives serve mainly as protection against decay. Many have no effect on appearance. Those that do usually leave a discoloration that requires covering with paint or stain. One, creosote, leaves a discoloration that cannot be covered.

Finishes—usually paints or stains—protect against weathering. Some do double duty as guards against decay. These do affect appearance, changing color, hiding wood grain, sometimes even hiding wood texture.

The degree of protection and the type (or types) of finish you may need for your deck depend on climate, grade and species of wood, intensity of deck use, and any esthetic factors you have in mind. More specifically, fungi and bacteria flourish where humidity keeps wood moist, or constant exposure to water keeps it wet; checking, splitting, warping, and related problems come from severe weather (especially cold). Species and grades of wood vary in their resistance to damage from weathering and use. They also vary in appearance. (See the chart on page 95.)

This chapter describes the major types of preservatives and finishes, giving their most effective uses.

Descriptions of preservatives come first because many must be applied *before* the deck is constructed, also because they go on as primers under finishes.

## Preservatives

All preservatives do double duty. They keep moisture out of wood so fungi and bacteria cannot nourish themselves from it (and to minimize weather damage), and they carry toxins that inhibit growth of decay-causing organisms.

## Pentachlorophenol

Pentachlorophenol, in various forms, is one of the proven wood preservatives.

Most commonly, it comes as the preservative in commercial water repellent preservatives. In their clear form, these compounds are the most effective preservatives for decks left in their natural wood hues. (They also come with tints.)

Preservatives containing pentachlorophenol do not prevent the absorption of water, but retard the rate at which the moisture content of wood changes when exposed to frequent shifts from dry to wet, whether from rain or high humidity. They are not as effective if constantly subject to water or high humidity. (The pentachlorophenol protects only against decay caused by fungi or bacteria; other components in the solution protect against moisture-induced weathering.)

Recommended for use alone, or as primers for stained or painted decks, these solutions can be applied by brushing, dipping, or soaking. Soaking is the more effective technique, and should be used for substructure members in all climates, for all members in damp regions or ones with severe winters. No matter which technique, take special care to soak all ends.

Water repellent preservatives are applied before construction. However, any trimming done during or after construction requires heavy brushing of the solution onto fresh cuts.

Wear gloves and cover clothing while working with pentachlorophenol. It is mildly toxic, and even dangerous around mouth and eyes. Work outdoors.

If any of the compound is left over, store it in glass jars away from sunlight.

Deck surfaces should have a new brushed application every second year.

Pentachlorophenol also can serve as an alternative to creosote if applied at a mill by pressure treatment. In this form, it discolors the wood, will rub off the surface, and has a lingering unpleasant odor—but can be painted over, an advantage over creosote. Wood pressure-treated with pentachlorophenol should be used only for in-ground or in-water posts or pilings. (It is effective only in fresh water, not salt.)

## Copper naphthenate

Applied by brushing, dipping, or soaking, copper naphthenate is almost as effective as pentachlorophenol, and can be used for nearly the same purposes.

Dark green, it leaves a green tinge on treated wood. This can be covered with two coats of paint.

Although using copper naphthenate eliminates the possibility of a natural wood finish, the material is not toxic to plants or animals, a quality which makes it especially useful for treating the insides of planters.

## Creosote

Long-used, well-proven creosote is at once a water repellent and a preservative. A product of coal tar, it is mildly toxic to plants and animals and also is insoluble in water.

Its use on decks is limited to underpinnings, and more especially to posts or pilings immersed in water (salt or fresh) or buried in earth. This is because it stains black, and cannot be coated with paint. Another limitation is a lingering aroma which few find pleasant.

Although creosote can be brushed on, or applied by dipping or soaking, it is by far at its most effective if wood is pressure-treated with it. With the latter method, a creosoted post or piling may last 40 years and more.

## Water-borne salt preservatives

Water-borne salts applied to wood by pressure treatment are clean and odorless, but leave a light yellow, green, blue green, or brownish tinge, depending on the exact chemical composition of the salts.

These preservatives are highly recommended by experts. Their main limitation is that they should be covered by paints or solid color stains to hide the discoloration.

Wood pressure-treated with these nonleachable salts is widely available, although difficult to find in some regions. (Where not available, it can be obtained by special order through local building suppliers. The trade offs are expense versus reliable durability.)

Standard water-borne salt preservatives include Acid Copper Chromate (ACC), Ammoniacal Copper Arsenate (ACA), Chromated Copper Arsenate (CCA), Chromated Zinc Chloride (CZA), and Fluor Chrome Arsenate Phenol (FCAP).

All of the water-borne salt preservatives can be used for lumber above grade. Other uses are specific.

For use in water, choose ACA or CCA.

For use in the ground, choose ACC, ACA, or CCA.

All of the water-borne salts can be

## Applying preservatives

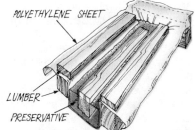

POLYETHYLENE SHEET

LUMBER

PRESERVATIVE

TROUGH CAN BE MADE FOR ALL SIZE LUMBER

PARTIALLY FILLED WITH PRESERVATIVE, A 50 GALLON DRUM IS HANDY FOR SOAKING SHORT LUMBER & POSTS

applied to wood only by pressure treatment. The wood should be dry before being stained or painted. A greenish gray powder may be present on wood surfaces at delivery. This can be swept away easily.

## Finishes

Finishes differ from preservatives in that they are deliberate choices for altering the natural appearance of wood.

Also, all preservatives penetrate the wood, while some finishes—notably paint—form a film around it.

It is recommended that finishes be underlain by preservatives for maximum protection of a deck.

### Bleaches

Bleaching is an economical and effective way to achieve rapid and uniform weathering of a deck.

Some trade-offs are involved in using bleach. It is most effective when applied to lumber *not* treated with a water repellent, which means some sacrifice in preserving or some loss of desired color effect.

In humid climates, a better choice might be a stain that produces a weathered look; see below.

If you wish to use a bleach on wood treated with a water repellent, wait 60 days after the treatment before applying the bleach; penetration will be more effective than on newly treated wood.

Apply one or two coats of bleach with a thick brush, taking care to avoid drip or lap marks. The surface must be clean and dry for application. However, once the deck is covered, periodic spraying with a hose will speed up the bleaching action. Follow the manufacturer's directions on when to wet the surface.

### Stains

Stains bridge the gap between natural finishes and paints, providing more color than the one, less than the other.

Within themselves, stains come in two color intensities. Semi-transparent types contain enough pigment to tint the wood surface, but not enough to hide the natural grain. Solid color stains contain more pigment, many of them appearing to be almost as opaque as paint. But stains do not cover the texture of the wood because they penetrate rather than forming a film as paint does.

Stains come in a variety of colors ranging from pale gray through the darkest wood colors. Paint and building supply stores keep sample chips indicating colors. However, these can give only a general idea. How your choice performs depends on your wood and your weather.

Stains must be selected carefully for technical as well as esthetic reasons. They come as both oil and water-based types. Experts recommend against water-based semi-transparent stains because they are difficult to refinish. Look for types labeled as "sealer-type" or "non-chalking." Others, not suited to heavy wear, may rub off onto clothing, or track into the house. The stain should contain a mildewcide.

A recommended deck staining method is to pretreat the lumber with clear water repellent, then apply stain after the structure has been up about a month. (As in the case of bleaches, stain will penetrate better with this or a longer wait after the water repellent has been applied.)

Heavy-bodied stains may be either brushed or sprayed on. Light-bodied types are sprayed on, then brushed smooth. (Also, light-bodied types can be applied in two coats using a brush only.)

In general, staining works best on rough or saw-textured lumber. On any surface, stains may require periodic refinishing because of wear or weathering.

### Paints

Paints require more work to apply than natural finishes, need more maintenance, and are more costly. However, they can do some things natural finishes cannot: create solid color effects from muted to vibrant, and permit use of lower grades of lumber in the decking since their opaque quality masks defects.

Paints divide into two general classes, oil-based and water-based. Both are suitable for general above-grade use.

Alkyds are the most commonly used oil-based paints today. They are durable, and do not have the unwelcome aromas of older linseed oil-based types. (Some alkyds are described on the label as alkyd-resin paints; the resin has nothing to do with the oil base, but serves as a drying agent.)

Acrylic latex paints are the water-based type best suited to covering decks.

Two particular points need noting:

• Alkyd paints come in gloss, semi-gloss, and flat finishes. The semi-gloss and flat finishes are not recommended for some wood species since they tend to absorb moisture that might lead to decay.

• Latex paints can be applied over either oil-based or water-based primers in many applications. In the section below there is a general recommendation to use oil-based primers. In the cases of redwood and western red cedar, this is absolutely imperative. Water-based primers may dissolve extractives in the wood, leading to discoloration of the paint.

For the longest lasting finish, pretreat the lumber with water repellent and apply the primer before erecting the deck. Wait two or more days between soaking the wood in water repellent and applying the primer. Primer should cover all lumber surfaces when in place, including the inner faces of built-up posts, beams, or joists (see page 75). Apply two topcoats after the deck is completed.

Regardless of the paint type used for the topcoat, the primer should be an oil-based paint with pigments *not* containing zinc oxide. Special attention should be paid to the chemical compatibility of the water repellent, primer, and topcoat. Be sure that the manufacturer's recommendations apply specifically to the kinds of treatment and finish you are using. Using materials all from the same manufacturer is a head start on compatibility, but labels must be checked to assure workable combinations even so.

Because heat may create drying problems and dust, leading to marred or roughened surfaces, try to paint on a cool, windless day. In hot, dry weather, paint only after the sun is low so drying can be slow.

Before priming or painting, always sweep or dust surfaces, and be sure they are dry. If the wood is painted while moist, the paint may fail to bond, leading to blistering or other failure.

Paint may be applied with either brush or roller.

## Clear film finishes

Resin-based sealers, varnishes, and synthetics (polyurethanes) that form a clear film on wood surfaces are not recommended for general use on decks. Because they do not form tight bonds, such films may crack and peel from weathering over periods as short as a year. Refinishing demands tedious scraping, sanding, or application of chemical removers.

## Waterproof finishes

For decks that must be watertight owing to location on rooftops, several finishes exist. All require professional application, and are formidable tasks even for skilled workers.

The main choices are these:

**Elastomeric coatings.** Various neoprene, silicone, and rubber-based finishes go by the general name of elastomeric coatings. They form watertight elastic membranes. Tough and skid-resistant, elastomerics come in a modest range of colors.

**Epoxy resin finishes.** These are applied in three coats, roughly at two-hour intervals. They can be pigmented with dry mineral oxides, or dry, clean aggregate can be mixed to give a pebbly appearance. Typical coatings (applied with brush, squeegee, or roller) are 1/8 to 1/4 inch thick. Plywood is the usual subfloor.

## Maintenance problems

All finishes are subject to deterioration over time. The process can be hastened by poor maintenance.

Most of the serious problems stem from low quality materials, faults in the deck design, or careless application of the finish itself.

### Dirt

Inevitably, people using a deck track pebbles, dirt, or other abrasives onto it. Unless a deck is cleaned regularly, the resulting abrasion will wear away both finishes and wood fiber. The recommended cleaning program is a regular scrubbing with a bristle brush and mild detergent, followed by a hose rinse.

### Mildew

A fungus that attacks wood surfaces when both air and moisture are present, mildew first appears as dark spots that may be mistaken for dirt. If undisturbed, the spots gradually fan out into large areas of gray, black, or dark brown.

To remove the spots or small areas on natural finishes or painted surfaces, scrub the mildew with a household detergent or mild cleanser and rinse with laundry bleach.

Large mildewed areas should be scrubbed with a solution of 1 cup of trisodium phosphate and 1 cup of household liquid bleach mixed with 1 gallon of warm water. Rinse thoroughly with a 1:1 solution of water and household bleach. Allow the deck to dry naturally, then treat it again with the original finish or with touchup paint containing mildewcide.

### Surface bleeding

Moisture or pitch in unseasoned or improperly finished lumber can cause surface bleeding. Bleeding discolors natural finishes and breaks through paint film. Beads of pitch may be removed by scraping then rubbing the residue with a rag and turpentine. Bleeding stains caused by moisture can be washed off natural finishes with water and household detergent.

Stubborn spots may require trisodium phosphate solution (see "Mildew," preceding) followed by this oxalic acid treatment:

Dissolve 4 ounces of oxalic acid crystals in 1 gallon of water in a glass or plastic container; apply with a cloth or soft brush. Rinse the treated surface thoroughly *after* the solution has dried. Warning: oxalic acid is poisonous and hazardous to skin, eyes, clothing, and plants. Wear rubber gloves; pour leftover solution down the drain; thoroughly wash containers, gloves, cloths, and brushes.

### Nail stains

Copper and poorly galvanized common steel nails may cause nail stains when exposed to moisture. Redwood, cedar, and cypress are particularly susceptible to stain. The problem can be avoided if you use stainless steel, aluminum, or fine-quality hot-dipped galvanized nails in the original construction.

Nail stains are difficult to remove because they penetrate deeply and recur if corroding nails are not replaced. If you find only a few nail stains, you can countersink the offending nails well below the surface, swab the holes with a water repellent, and fill the holes with a non-oily wood filler for natural finishes or with putty for painted surfaces. Oxalic acid (see "Surface bleeding," preceding) may remove the remaining nail stain from natural finishes. Touch up all painted surfaces.

### Splash lines

Marks occur on natural finishes where water splashes persistently. Typical causes include runoff from eaves, garden sprinklers, puddles, and swimming pool splash. This type of uneven wetting stains natural finishes and makes paint deteriorate rapidly. The best way to avoid splash lines is to keep an eye out for the sources of the problem and correct them. Installing a new gutter or repairing an old one can solve a problem with eaves. A solid screen might stop splashes from a swimming pool.

If a mechanical solution is impractical, hose down the entire surface regularly to even out the stains.

# LIVING WITH YOUR DECK

**For maximum livability, consider**

- **practical & decorative lighting**
- **water for people & plants**
- **ways to warm the deck**

An unfurnished deck is like an empty stage. You set the scene by dressing the set and adding props for activities. Among the possible additions are water, lights, heat, game courts, and storage.

Chefs particularly, and music buffs enjoy having a little electricity at hand. Electrical power can run a barbecue spit, power night lights, and provide the juice for a stereo. Sunbathers and gardeners have a different need—water. A bit of plumbing can provide outdoor showers and gardenside sinks and faucets. This chapter concerns readying your deck for many roles. You spark the performance by adding any or all of the features discussed.

Be aware, though, that adding electrical power or water to a deck can add many dollars to the cost.

A general recommendation is to live with your deck for several months before deciding which extras will serve you best. As patterns of use evolve, they will make many of the decisions almost automatic. For the owners of most decks, the wait imposes no penalties, for electric, gas, or water lines can be added at any time. Some low-level and most masonry decks are exceptions; utilities may have to be installed during their construction.

## Electrical wiring

Electricity has the greatest impact on day-to-day deck use. Even a simple circuit with only one or two outlets can expand the deck's usefulness by adding power for outdoor lights, rotisserie cooking, music, television, and more.

Two types of systems can be used outdoors: 110-volt circuits connected directly to the main power system box of the house, and a 12-volt transformer system plugged into a 110-volt convenience outlet. Electrical installation for 110-volt circuits, however, presents three problems: relatively high cost, very strict code regulations, and quite often the need for professional help. A 12-volt system is much safer for children and pets, and code regulations are minimal.

## 110-volt circuits

Any 110-volt wiring diagrams outside the regular house circuits should be prepared professionally. The completed plans (including connection details and material specifications) should be checked by your local building department. If you have not had house-wiring experience, hire a professional electrician to do the job. Installation of 110-volt circuits is strictly regulated by codes. In addition, the work requires special skills and tools and can be dangerous for the inexperienced.

## 12-volt systems

Low-voltage systems are easier to install, somewhat lower in cost, and less rigidly controlled by codes than 110-volt circuitry. They may be purchased packaged specifically for the do-it-yourselfer, or a lighting expert can put your system together. Since the development of sophisticated camper equipment, low-voltage systems can now provide many of the amenities formerly powered only by 110-volt systems: lights, television, tape decks, refrigeration, and so forth. However, the equipment must be specially designed for low-voltage operations; your indoor appliances cannot be converted.

**Designing low-voltage circuits.** The best place to get advice on designing a low-voltage system for your deck is a retail electrical store. Basically, a low-voltage circuit consists of a transformer connected to a regular house circuit. It converts the house's 110 volts A.C. to 12 volts D.C. (the same power available from 12-volt automobile batteries). The transformer's wattage capacity determines the size and length of wiring the circuit can have and the number of appliances or fixtures that can be attached. Generally, the circuits are designed for transformers of 100 to 250-watt capacities. If yours will have a greater load, use separate circuits (each with its own transformer).

A transformer should have a grounded shield between primary and secondary windings to prevent

110-volt leakage into the 12-volt circuit. A 6-foot length of cord to plug into the 110-volt house outlet is usually provided with a transformer. Warning: Adding extension cords can increase resistance beyond proper limits, causing transformer failure. Outdoor outlets must be the grounded, exterior type that meet electrical code requirements.

The cord used for the secondary supply line from the transformer should be stranded, two-wire No. 12 (or heavier), not exceeding 100 feet in total lengths. Each fixture usually is supplied with a 25-foot long cable which clips to the No. 12 supply line. A typical 12-volt bulb draws about 18 watts, so a 100-watt transformer could power six lights, a 250-watt transformer could handle 14. Unlike cord for 110-volt circuits, low-voltage wiring in most areas can legally be strung overhead, stapled to outside walls or deck structurals, laid on top of or buried under the ground without conduit, or installed without junction boxes or other special protective devices.

## Lighting

Deck illumination falls into two categories: functional and decorative. Both functional and decorative lighting can either be permanently installed or set up temporarily for special occasions. Electricity is the most common source for permanent light, but gas is novel, and for some situations it is effective. Among the alternatives for temporary or special-occasion lighting are torches, kerosene lanterns, and gas mantle lights. These require special safety precautions.

Following are some guides to deck lighting.

## Functional lighting

Functional deck lighting is used for general illumination; concentrated lighting is used for specific activities and for safe-lighting steps and other underfoot hazards.

Unless you have the help of a lighting expert, plan to install your lighting (including wiring, if possible) after your deck is completed

and in use. Identify your needs by spending time on the deck after dark. Then, on your construction drawings (see page 24), mark areas where light would be helpful.

**General illumination.** Keep two factors in mind when planning your functional deck lighting: first, outdoor lighting requires far less illumination than indoor lighting; and second, all lamps should be located where they will not shine straight into people's eyes.

You can use any of several methods to keep lights from shining into eyes. One is to conceal lamps behind wall valances, overhead rafters, or roof eaves. Another method is to bounce light from low-level sources off the house wall, screens, or other large vertical surfaces next to the deck. A third technique is to mount floodlights from about 10 to 25 feet overhead (off roof eaves or in trees) in positions casting light onto the deck at about a 45° angle.

As a general rule, consistent with uniform illumination, use the fewest bulbs of the highest possible wattage. A single fixture with a 200-watt bulb is cheaper both to install and to operate than two fixtures with 100-watt bulbs.

**Concentrated lighting.** Areas used for nighttime activities—game courts, outdoor workbenches, and barbecues—should have brighter lighting than general area illumination.

For versatile activity lighting, you can buy portable, telescoping stands (at most photographic supply stores) for mounting floodlights. They provide easily adjustable lighting and can be stored when not in use. If you decide on portable lighting, be sure to include plenty of convenience outlets in your wiring plan. Try to limit the length of portable lamp cords to 6 feet or less: short cords eliminate tangled wires underfoot and reduce the possibility of bulbs dimming from voltage drops in 12-volt systems.

**Safety lights.** For safety lights along pathways or stairs, only low levels of illumination are needed. Be sure that the lighting itself creates no hazards. It should throw no deceptive shadows, nor should it glare or be an obstacle to trip over. Low mushroom-type lights or recessed lamps and backlighting from beneath steps or deck edges are typical solutions. It's difficult to position high lights so that they won't glare or make people walk in their own shadows.

### Decorative lighting

Permanent dramatic illumination of deck area plantings or trees, and temporary festive lighting for special occasions are the most common functions of decorative lighting. Electric lighting is best for permanent use; a variety of sources can offer occasional lighting.

**Landscape illumination.** The nighttime character of a deck can be dramatically enhanced by selective illumination of an adjacent garden, tree branches overhead, or plants on the deck. Positioning of outdoor floodlights (see "Lighting equipment," below) will create the desired effect. To come up with the best arrangement for your deck, experiment.

One temporary approach is to use heavy-duty extension cords (weatherproof and grounded) as movable power sources before installing permanent wiring. If you plan to use a low-voltage system, start experimenting with a couple of 25-watt PAR 36 floodlights. For 110-volt lighting, begin with an assortment of bulbs ranging from 50 to 150 watts. For the handiest trial-and-error placements, use clamp-on lamps.

As you try different arrangements, follow these guidelines:
• Position lights so that they are concealed as much as possible during the daytime.
• Test each effect by viewing it not only from the deck but also from inside the house and from outside, where neighbors or passers-by will see the light.
• Try different effects, including silhouetting, uplighting, downlighting, fill lighting, and diffusing.

**Color lighting.** Bizarre and surprising results can come from haphazard use of color lighting. For example, green light is best for accenting foliage but turns facial complexions to gruesome hues and makes most food appear unappetizing; yellow light gives warmth to brown house siding but makes green landscaping look dead.

Without expert knowledge, the safest approach is to limit colorful illumination to deck fountains or water sprays and amber lighting to decorative ponds with still water.

**Festive lighting.** Holidays, parties, and celebrations often call for temporary festive lighting on a deck. If you plan to wire your deck for electricity, anticipate these lighting needs by installing a generous number of convenience outlets around the deck perimeters. And consider placing at least one or two outlets in overhead locations, such as tree branches, roof rafters, and eaves. The cost of adding these outlets is relatively low if they are included in the original wiring.

Decorative lighting can be created from strings of lights especially designed for outdoor use (do not use the indoor type). Miniature lights can ornament a deck umbrella rim or food service table, or even form a "Welcome" sign. Strings of larger bulbs make good light sources for paper lanterns or for do-it-yourself party lanterns. Or you can try concealing bulbs behind deck railings or below deck edges to create a floating effect.

Fire safety is one of the major concerns with nonelectric decorative lighting. Hawaiian luau torches and other types of flares should be securely held in place by cleats or brackets that have been nailed or screwed to the deck. Take extreme care to locate any open flame where it won't be accidentally touched or brushed against by clothing. Candle-powered lanterns are less hazardous but still require care so that the heat from their chimneys does not ignite paper decorations or other flammable material.

### Lighting equipment

Outdoor fixtures come in hundreds of shapes, sizes, and prices, but electric bulbs are limited to a few basic types. In approximate order of decreasing intensity, they are:

Tungsten-halogen ("quartz")
Mercury vapor
PAR Lamps (automobile "sealed-beam" type)
Fluorescent
Common glass-enclosed filament bulbs

PAR and filament bulbs are available to use with either 110-volt or low-voltage systems; the others usually are designed only for 110-volt circuits.

Emitted light's range of brilliancy and color may be different for each of these types. The angle that the light covers also varies. For example, a 150-watt filament bulb in a reflector mounted 16 feet above the deck and aimed at a 45° angle will light an area of 467 square feet; a 150-watt PAR lamp in the same position will light only 231 square feet. Fluorescent bulbs give diffused light; for general illumination, the light from other types of bulbs is usually diffused by frosted glass, canvas, or other opaque coverings. PAR bulbs may be used in exposed sockets; other types must be in weatherproof units especially designed for outdoor use.

To meet your deck's particular lighting needs, consult suppliers specializing in outdoor illumination equipment.

**Gaslight.** If your home has natural gas service, you might consider gaslights for general deck illumination. Mantle-type lamps in a variety of fixture designs are available through some outdoor lighting retailers. Typical single-mantle units emit light equal to that of a 60-watt filament bulb; double-mantle lamps, the equivalent of 100-watt filament bulbs. Torch-type gas fixtures are also available for decorative purposes, but their cheerful flames cast too little light for general illumination.

Mantle-type lamps, with glass globes, are usually designed to operate 24 hours a day. This round-the-clock feature makes excellent security light for protection from prowlers but it does waste energy. Operation costs vary from area to area, depending on the cost of natural gas. Professional installation is comparable in cost to professional electrical wiring; consult the utility company that provides your gas service.

## Heating a deck

Effectively heating your deck can make it comfortable to use in no-wind temperatures as low as 50°. Heating devices work on the same principle as the sun—the area is warmed by heat radiating from the source, rather than by heated air. Artificial deck heat is radiated by infrared heaters (gas-operated or electric) or fire (in braziers or fireplaces).

### Infrared heaters

Gas and electrical infrared heaters are the most effective sources for artificially heating decks. Weatherproof wall and overhead units are available for fixed installation and as freestanding, portable models. They must be aimed at the objects being heated; the area they will cover depends on their location and their rated heat emission in BTUs (British Thermal Units).

**Electrically operated heaters.** Infrared heaters operated by electricity are of two equally effective types: quartz tube and glassplate. Both are available for 110-volt or 220-volt operation (requiring a special circuit). They are heavy power users, using from 1,000 to 3,000 watts. Large 220-volt units produce about 10,000 BTUs per hour.

**Gas-operated.** Having a higher rated heat-emission range than electric models, gas-type infrared heaters can operate on household gas mains or separate propane systems. The former are designed for fixed installation or made semiportable by flexible gas lines attached to special fittings on the house gas system. Propane-operated units are completely portable and range in heat ratings up to 50,000 BTUs per hour, equal to the output of a small house furnace. Typically, a large propane unit can burn at full

capacity for 10 hours or more on 25 pounds of fuel (propane is held for use under pressure as a liquid and becomes a gas for burning when released in the heater; it is sold by liquid weight, 4.45 pounds equaling 1 gallon). Propane heating costs are comparable to household gas heating, but propane use requires making trips to a dealer for refills.

### Fire heat sources

Movable braziers, permanent fireplaces, and firepits (for ground-hugging decks only) are usually more attractive than infrared heaters but not as effective. Normally, fireplaces and firepits must be planned and installed during deck construction. Because their foundations must rest on the ground, they are difficult to build for decks that rise more than a few feet above grade level. To get a better idea of methods for adapting fireplaces and firepits to low-level decks, see the *Sunset* book *Fireplaces*.

## Pipes for water

Plumbing ranks in importance with electric wiring as a deck convenience. At least one hose connection is necessary for easy deck maintenance; more extensive plumbing can make numerous other features possible, adding comfort and convenience to the deck.

### Deck water uses

In addition to many of its normal indoor household uses, water has some uniquely outdoor uses for gardening, fountains, decorative ponds, tank swimming pools, outdoor showers, and fire protection.

**Hose outlets.** A basic requirement for easy deck maintenance and container gardening is one or more hose outlets. Faucets and hoses can be effectively camouflaged in storage boxes recessed below the deck. One about 3 by 5 feet makes a handy place to store from 50 to 100 feet of hose. Hinges and handles should be recessed below walking surfaces to avoid tripping passers-by. Be sure to

make the lid chain long enough so that the hatch will stay open when the chain is fully extended. You can also conceal a faucet and hose in a bench with solid sides and a hinged seat or in a workbench with vertical doors.

**Planter sprinklers.** Plant wells and built-in planters are easily fitted with permanent sprinklers or misting heads. Concealed pipes may run through the bottom or sides of planters below decking. Noncorroding plastic pipe is recommended for that part of a water line that is buried in the earth of the wells or planters. Sprinklers may be controlled manually with a valve or installed with a clock-activated device that automatically turns them on and off at set times.

The spike-type sprinkler head commonly used with hoses can be used for tubs and planters that are occasionally moved. Insert the spike in a tight-fitting 1-inch-deep hole drilled in the side of the planter, adjacent decking, a post, or another wood structural. If the spike is too long, you can always trim it with a hacksaw.

**Outdoor showers and sinks.** Two of the most useful indoor-type water fixtures adapted to decks are showers and sinks. Cold water service is adequate, but the addition of hot water makes a shower or sink a real luxury.

Typically, a shower is for a deck near the beach or swimming pool; a built-in sink is usually part of the barbecue scene. But these conveniences can be used for other purposes. When pointed down, an adjustable shower head mounted 3½ feet above the deck (instead of the customary 5 feet 8 inches) is just the right height for cleaning muddy feet or boots, sit-down shampooing, or washing pets. Pointed up or out, it is an ideal "playing in the hose" substitute for youngsters and a quick cooler for sunbathers. Built-in deck sinks can be equally useful for meeting the outdoor washup needs of gardeners, mudpie makers, finger painters, ceramicists, or even the family automobile mechanic. Sink height at the rim should be 3 feet 1 inch for adults and 2 feet

7 inches for children. Be sure to include a generous counter area and enclose the plumbing underneath with exterior plywood or appropriate cabinet material.

Fixture suppliers can give you advice on available equipment and methods of installation.

**Fountains and sprays.** The sound and sight of moving water in a fountain or spray adds vitality to a deck. In addition, the motion contributes to climate control in hot weather.

Mechanically, both of these devices work on the same water-saving principle: water is sprayed into the air and recirculated through an open reservoir by an electric pump. Water loss is limited to modest evaporation.

Installations range widely in terms of cost and sophistication. Commonly available submersible pump sizes, for example, run from tiny 1/55 horsepower models spouting water 2 feet high at a rate of 135 gallons per hour to husky units lifting 675 gallons per hour 12 feet high. Non-submersible motor systems are also used frequently.

The simplest type for the do-it-yourselfer to handle comes in a kit. Usually a kit will include a small submersible pump and a plastic reservoir or heavy gauge polyethylene sheet for forming a pool. Flexible tubing and simple fountainheads may also be part of the package. The assembled fountains are usually small enough to be moved and to create no water-weight problems (see below).

For extensive details on the subject, see the *Sunset* book *Garden Pools, Fountains & Waterfalls*. Also, if you are considering more elaborate water systems than those provided by kits, consult a specialist.

**Decorative pools and bathing tanks.** The first consideration in planning any deck feature that holds water is water's formidable weight—about 62.4 pounds per cubic foot (for every square foot, 5.2 pounds per inch of depth) or 8⅓ pounds per gallon. For example, the water in a modest pool 4 feet square by 2 feet deep will weight approximately 2,000 pounds. Even a child's small wading pool will weigh more than 1,000 pounds when filled. Given below are some rules to follow.

Consult an engineer if you plan to add any medium sized or large ponds or pools (or a number of smaller ones); he or she will tell you whether or not you must strengthen the deck substructure. A support system for a swimming tank should always be independent of the deck's substructure.

A decorative pool or pond is easy to add to a completed deck if fill-and-drain plumbing was installed before the deck was completed. A pond or pool may be as functional as it is decorative: catching splashes under eaves, separating different activity areas, protecting outward-opening casement windows, providing seating (on a particularly wide rim).

Small ponds only 6 to 8 inches deep can display an amazing variety of aquatic planting, inexpensive goldfish, and other animate or inanimate objects of interest. (Goldfish feed on mosquitoes and other insects; they will reproduce but will not survive heavy winter freezes unless several feet of water remains unfrozen beneath the ice.)

Adding swimming pools to decks is beyond the scope of this book except as noted above. For a full discussion of the possibilities, see the *Sunset* book *Swimming Pools*.

**Fire hydrants.** If your deck tops a slope covered with brush or wild grass in a high fire hazard area, seriously consider adding a concealed fire hydrant to the deck's plumbing. Brush or grass fires tend to burn rapidly upslope for long distances. Decks can trap superheated air rushing ahead of the fire, attracting the fire to the house. (In some communities, decks are prohibited because of this hazard.)

The first step is to consult your fire department and then the utility company supplying your water. If you install a hydrant, also invest in a canvas firehose with a fire-fighting nozzle. (Your fire department may sell or give you an outdated hose; periodic hose replacement is required of most fire departments.) Locate the hydrant so that the hose can remain attached and laid out in 15 to 20-foot coils ready for use. The line for the hydrant should be as large as the water supply line to the house and should be connected directly to it.

The addition of a hydrant may reduce the premium cost of your home's fire insurance.

## Plumbing installation

Water piping systems for decks are comparable in cost to electric wiring. They are also subject to building code regulations in most areas. If you are short on plumbing experience, plan and budget for professional help. Inviting bids on the job from qualified plumbers is a recommended cost-saving practice. Protecting the pipes against freezing presents further complications, especially for decks built well above grade level.

**When to install plumbing.** For a high-level deck with access to its underside, install pipes after completing the deck. Use the deck long enough beforehand to know where and how you will want to use water. Installing an entire system at one time is less costly than developing it bit by bit.

Low-level decks with limited or no access underneath must usually have the plumbing installed before the deck surface is laid. This is particularly important if pipes must be buried underground or, where exposed, be insulated or otherwise protected against winter freezes.

**Protecting the pipe.** Deck pipes are especially vulnerable to bursting during freezing temperatures. Main pipes buried beneath the frost line are protected. Short lengths of exposed pipe leading up to deck faucets can be insulated. Extensive piping attached to beams or joists should be completely drained in winter. A safe plan is to equip the system with a main cutoff valve inside the house and a drain valve (or threaded plug) at the lowest point in the deck plumbing. During winter, shut the main valve and keep the drain valve open or the plug removed. Open all faucets or other fixtures and drain any sink traps.

# Hardware & Lumber Guide: What to buy, how to use

## Nails

Use a nail that is three times as long as the thickness of the board you are nailing. Nails with sharp points hold better than blunt ones, but tend to split wood, so flatten the point with a hammer before driving into easily split wood. For weather resistance, use aluminum, stainless steel, or hot-dipped galvanized nails. To increase resistance to withdrawal, use nails with zinc or cement coatings, or use ring or spiral nails. Nail sizes in the chart below are indicated by "penny," abbreviated as "d"; for example, a 20-penny nail is known as 20d nail.

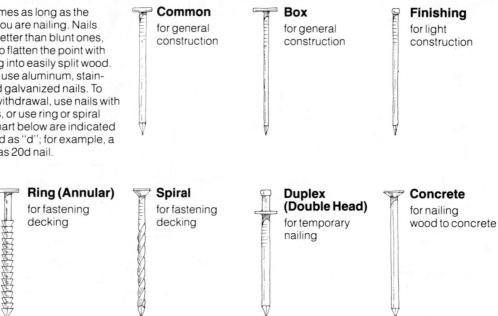

**Common** for general construction

**Box** for general construction

**Finishing** for light construction

**Casing** for trim

**Ring (Annular)** for fastening decking

**Spiral** for fastening decking

**Duplex (Double Head)** for temporary nailing

**Concrete** for nailing wood to concrete

## Nails: Lengths, Diameters & Numbers per Pound

| Penny Size | Length (inches) | Common Nails Diameter (inches) | Common Nails Number per Pound | Box & Casing Nails Diameter (inches) | Box & Casing Nails Number per Pound | Finishing Nails Diameter (inches) | Finishing Nails Number per Pound |
|---|---|---|---|---|---|---|---|
| 2d | 1 | .072 | 876 | .069 | 1010 | .062 | 1351 |
| 3d | 1¼ | .083 | 568 | .078 | 635 | .069 | 807 |
| 4d | 1½ | .102 | 316 | .083 | 473 | .072 | 584 |
| 5d | 1¾ | .102 | 271 | .083 | 406 | .072 | 500 |
| 6d | 2 | .115 | 181 | .102 | 236 | .095 | 309 |
| 7d | 2¼ | .115 | 161 | .102 | 210 | .095 | 238 |
| 8d | 2½ | .131 | 106 | .115 | 145 | .102 | 189 |
| 9d | 2¾ | .131 | 96 | .115 | 132 | .102 | 172 |
| 10d | 3 | .148 | 69 | .127 | 94 | .115 | 121 |
| 12d | 3¼ | .148 | 63 | .127 | 88 | .115 | 113 |
| 16d | 3½ | .220 | 49 | .134 | 71 | .120 | 90 |
| 20d | 4 | .238 | 31 | .148 | 52 | .134 | 62 |
| 30d | 4½ | .259 | 24 | .148 | 46 | — | — |
| 40d | 5 | .284 | 18 | .165 | 35 | — | — |
| 50d | 5½ | — | 14 | — | — | — | — |
| 60d | 6 | — | 11 | — | — | — | — |

## Wood Screws

Use a screw that is long enough so ⅔ (*never* less than ½) of its length will enter base in which threads are embedded. Length should be about ⅛" less than combined thickness of boards being joined.

To install a wood screw, drill a *clearance hole* for the shank (the threadless part) and a *pilot hole* for the threaded portion (see chart on next page). Flathead screws should be countersunk, either flush with or below the surface of the wood. When wood plugs are used to cover countersunk screws, plug holes must also be drilled.

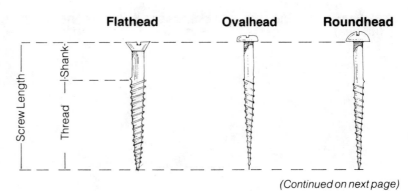

Flathead    Ovalhead    Roundhead

*(Continued on next page)*

## Wood Screws: Available Lengths, plus Sizes of Clearance, Pilot & Plug Holes

| Screw No. | 0 | 1 | 2 | 3 | 4 | 5 | 6 | 7 | 8 | 9 | 10 | 11 | 12 | 14 | 16 | 18 | 20 |
|---|---|---|---|---|---|---|---|---|---|---|---|---|---|---|---|---|---|
| Available Lengths (inches) | ¼ | ¼ | ¼–½ | ¼–⅝ | ⅜–¾ | ⅜–¾ | ⅜–1½ | ⅜–1½ | ½–2 | ½–2¼ | ½–2¼ | ¾–2¼ | ⅞–2½ | 1–2¾ | 1¼–3 | 1½–4 | 1¾–4 |
| Clearance Hole (inches) | 1/16 | 5/64 | 3/32 | 7/64 | 7/64 | 1/8 | 9/64 | 5/32 | 11/64 | 3/16 | 3/16 | 13/64 | 7/32 | ¼ | 17/64 | 19/64 | 21/64 |
| Pilot Hole Softwood (inches) | 1/64 | 1/32 | 1/32 | 3/64 | 3/64 | 1/16 | 1/16 | 1/16 | 5/64 | 5/64 | 3/32 | 3/32 | 7/64 | 7/64 | 9/64 | 9/64 | 11/64 |
| Pilot Hole Hardwood (inches) | 1/32 | 1/32 | 3/64 | 1/16 | 1/16 | 5/64 | 5/64 | 3/32 | 3/32 | 7/64 | 7/64 | 1/8 | 1/8 | 9/64 | 3/32 | 3/16 | 13/64 |
| Bit Sizes for Plug Holes | — | — | 3 | 4 | 4 | 4 | 5 | 5 | 6 | 6 | 6 | 7 | 7 | 8 | 9 | 10 | 11 |

## Bolts

Length of bolt should equal total thickness of both pieces of lumber plus 1-inch. For lumber up to 2 inches, use ¼-inch-diameter bolts; for 3-inch-lumber, ⅜-inch bolts; for 4-inch lumber, ½-inch bolts. Drill hole 1/16 inch larger than diameter of bolt unless snug fit is essential. Use washer under both head and nut of machine bolt, under nut of carriage bolt.

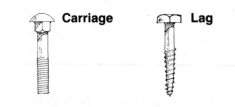

**Machine**     **Carriage**     **Lag**

### Bolts: Available Lengths*

| Bolt Diameter (inches) | Machine Bolt (inches) | Carriage Bolt (inches) | Lag Bolt (inches) |
|---|---|---|---|
| ¼ | ½–8 | ¾–8 | 1–6 |
| 5/16 | ½–8 | ¾–8 | 1–10 |
| ⅜ | ¾–12 | ¾–12 | 1–12 |
| 7/16 | ¾–12 | 1–12 | 1–12 |
| ½ | ¾–24 | 1–20 | 1–12 |
| 9/16 | 1–30 | 1–20 | 1½–16 |
| ⅝ | 1–30 | 1–20 | 1½–16 |
| ¾ | 1–30 | 1–20 | 2–16 |
| ⅞ | 1½–30 | — | 2–16 |
| 1 | 1½–30 | — | — |

*Length intervals for machine and carriage bolts: ¼" increments to 6"; ½" increments from 6½" to 12"; 1" increments 13" and over.*
*Length intervals for lag bolts: ½" increments to 8"; 1" increments 9" and over.*

### Masonry Anchors

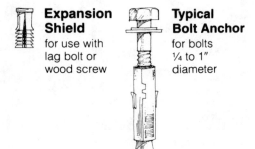

**Expansion Shield**
for use with lag bolt or wood screw

**Typical Bolt Anchor**
for bolts ¼ to 1" diameter

## Standard Dimensions of Surfaced Lumber

| Nominal Thickness (inches) | Width (inches) | Actual Thicknesses & Widths (inches) Surfaced Dry | Surfaced Unseasoned |
|---|---|---|---|
| 1 | 1 | ¾ | 25/32 |
| 2 | 2 | 1½ | 19/16 |
| — | 3 | 2½ | 29/16 |
| 4 | 4 | 3½ | 39/16 |
| 6 | 6 | 5½ | 5⅝ |
| | 8 | 7¼ | 7½ |
| — | 10 | 9¼ | 9½ |
| — | 12 | 11¼ | 11½ |

## Comparative Guide to Decking Lumber

| Species | Growing Range | Characteristics | Color | Average Weight | Recommended Finishes/ Preservatives |
|---|---|---|---|---|---|
| **Redwood** | Northwestern California, extreme Southwestern Oregon. | Known for its durability and natural resistance to decay, disease, and termites, especially among virgin-growth timber (second growth a little less durable); resists checking and warping; free from pitch, resins, and oils; moderately hard, strong, and stiff; medium nail-holding ability; holds finishes well; moderately easy to work. | *Heartwood:* light cherry to mahogany<br><br>*Sapwood:* cream to almost white | 28 lbs. per cubic foot | Needs no exterior finish; may be treated with water-repellant preservatives, bleaches, or light-bodied pigment stains, or painted; holds finishes very well; all-heart redwood needs no preservatives even for in-ground use. |
| **Western Red Cedar** | Pacific Northwest from Southern Alaska to Northern California; Washington east to Montana. | Similar to redwood in durability and resistance to decay and termites; high resistance, as well, to checking, weathering, and warping; free from resins; distinctive, pleasant aroma; moderately soft, somewhat weak and limber; moderate nail-holding ability; very easy to work. | *Heartwood:* reddish brown, light yellow<br><br>*Sapwood:* almost pure white | 23 lbs. per cubic foot | Needs no exterior finish; may be treated with water preservatives, bleaches, stains, or blister-resistant paints; absorbs and holds finishes well. |
| **Douglas Fir-Western Larch** | Western states (Rocky Mountains and Pacific Coast ranges); dense stands in Washington, Oregon. | Only heartwood is moderately decay-resistant; high proportion of heartwood; moderate resistance to cupping and twisting; resinous; moderately hard, wears well underfoot; very heavy, strong, and stiff; good nail-holding ability; somewhat difficult to work. | *Heartwood:* orange red, reddish brown<br><br>*Sapwood:* yellowish white | 33–38 lbs. per cubic foot | Preservative treatment recommended for exterior use; average ability to hold stains; below-average ability to hold paints. |
| **Southern Yellow Pine (Longleaf, Slash, Shortleaf, Loblolly)** | Southeastern U.S. from Maryland to Florida; Atlantic Coast to East Texas. | High resistance to decay and termites when pressure-treated with preservatives; heavier, harder, and more resinous than western pines; very strong and stiff; high resistance to blemishes and scars; moderate resistance to warping; good nail-holding ability; moderately easy to work. | *Heartwood:* reddish brown to orange<br><br>*Sapwood:* cream to lemon yellow | 36–43 lbs. per cubic foot | Should be pressure treated with preservatives for maximum durability, especially in moist and humid climates; below-average paint-holding ability. |
| **Eastern White, Northern, and Western Pine** | *Eastern and Northern Pine:* Maine to Northern Georgia, and across Great Lakes states.<br><br>*Western Pines (Idaho, Lodgepole, Ponderosa, and Sugar):* Western states. | Very light and soft woods with below-average resistance to decay and termites, but high resistance to warping; somewhat weak and limber; moderate nail-holding ability; easy to work. | *Heartwood:* cream, light reddish, orange, or light brown<br><br>*Sapwood:* almost white | 25–28 lbs. per cubic foot | Should be pressure treated with preservatives for maximum durability. Takes paints and stains very well. |
| **Eastern and Western Hemlock (Hem-Fir)** | *Eastern Hemlock:* Northeastern U.S. and along the Appalachians through Kentucky.<br><br>*Western Hemlock:* Northern Idaho, Montana, and along the Pacific Coast. | One of the least durable softwoods; fairly strong and stiff; nonresinous; wood resists checking, warping, and weathering well; below-average nail-holding properties; Western Hemlock moderately easy to work, Eastern somewhat more difficult. | *Heartwood:* reddish brown<br><br>*Sapwood:* buff | 29 lbs. per cubic foot | Should be well treated with preservatives before use; can take most oil or water-base preservatives and finishes; below-average paint-holding properties. |
| **Spruce (Engelmann, Eastern)** | *Engelmann:* Belts along the Cascade and Rocky Mountain ranges.<br><br>*Eastern (Red, White, and Black):* Maine through Wisconsin, Canada | Low in decay resistance; does not easily warp, split, or splinter; nonresinous; lightweight and soft-textured; moderately strong and stiff; good nail-holding properties; fairly easy to work. | *Heartwood and sapwood:* almost white to pale yellowish brown | 24 lbs. per cubic foot | Preservative recommended; can take most preservatives and finishes with proper application; good paint-holding properties. |

# INDEX

American Institute of Architects (AIA), 14
American Institute of Building Designers (AIBD), 14
American Society of Landscape Architects (ASLA), 14
Architects, 12–13
Architects' drawings, 9
Atriums, 59

Beams
  in substructure, 17
  seating, 78
  spans and spacings, 24–27
Benches, built-in, 28–29, 39, 44, 45, 46, 48, 49, 54, 55, 56, 59, 63, 64
Bench supports, securing, 28, 80
Bleach, as finish, 86
Bleeding, surface, 87
Blocking, 82
Board lumber, 16, 20
Bolts, 75–76, 94
Bowing, 20
Bracing (bridging), 25, 72, 79
Building codes, 5–6
Building permits, 6
Built-up structurals, 74–75

California Redwood Association, 21
Cantilevered decks, 11–12, 46, 50, 51
Changeable decks, 83
Checking, surface, 20, 84
Check list, deck builder's, 14
Climate, evaluating, 7–8
Concrete
  as deck surface, 16
  blocks, 19
  columns, 17–18, 74
  estimating, 67–69
  foundations, 15, 19, 25, 28, 67–69, 71–74
  mixing, 74
  ordering, 68–69
  piers, 19, 25, 28, 74
Construction, 70–83
Contour maps, 9
Contractors, 13–14
Contracts, 14
Copper naphthenate, 85
Creosote, 85
Cross bracing, 25, 78–79
Cupping, 16, 20
Cutting deck edges, 81–82

Deck Builder's Check List, 14
Decking
  laying, 72, 80–82
  materials, 15–21, 93–95
  spans, 24–26
Deed restrictions, 6
Design, 14, 22–31
Designers, 13
Dimension lumber, 16, 17, 18, 20, 23, 94
Do-it-yourself design/construction, 11
Drafters, 13
Drainage, 70–71

Easements, 6
Elastomeric coatings, 87
Elevation view, 23
Engawa-style decks, 43, 49
Engineers, 13
Entry decks, 34–35, 37, 42, 62
Epoxy resin finishes, 87

Fiberglass, 17
Finishes, deck, 86–87
Firepits, 38, 45
Flashing, 77
Flat grain, 20
Footings, 6, 25, 71, 72, 73–74
Foundations, 15, 18–19, 25, 28, 67–69, 71–74

Fountains, 92
Freestanding decks, 54–55

Garden rooms, 58–59
Gazebos, 55, 59
Grading, 71

Hardware, 19–20, 75–76, 93–94
Hardwood, 20
Heating, deck, 91
High-level decks, 5, 10–11, 30, 41, 48, 49, 50–51, 62
Hillside decks, 40–41, 42–43, 48–49, 64
Hot tubs, 39, 43, 53

Joists
  installing, 72, 78–79
  spacings and spans, 24–26

Kits, deck, 21
Knots, 20

Lag screws, 75–76, 93–94
Landscape architects, 12–13
Landscape designers, 13
Leakproof deck surfaces, 11
Ledger, fastening to house wall, 22, 72, 76–77
Levels, changing, 31
Lighting, deck, 35, 59, 89–91
Loads and heights, deck, 24
Location, choosing, 6–8
Low-level decks, 4–5, 10, 31, 33, 34, 36–37, 38–39, 44–45, 46–47, 52–53, 54–55, 56–57, 58–59, 72
Low-voltage wiring, 89
Lumber, 16, 17, 20–21, 23–24, 67, 68, 94–95
  imperfections, 20

Maintenance, 87
Materials
  estimating, 66–69
  list, sample, 69
  ordering, 68–69
  salvaged, 68
Metal connectors, 19
Mildew, 87
Modular decking, 83

Nails and nailing, 19, 81, 87, 93
National Oceanic and Atmospheric Administration (NOAA), 7
Nonskid deck surfaces, 17
North, finding, 9

Outdoor carpeting, 17
Overheads, deck, 28, 29–30, 37, 44, 46, 48, 49, 54, 55, 58, 59, 61, 80
Overhead supports, securing, 28, 80

Paints, 86–87
Passage width, 30
Pentachlorophenol, 85
Piers, 19, 25, 28, 71, 72, 73–74
Piling, as substructure, 17
Planning, deck, 4–14
Plans, drawing, 22–23
Plot plans, 9
Plumbing, 91–92
Plywood, exterior, 16, 24, 67, 81
Poles, as substructure, 17, 18
Pools
  decking around, 49, 53, 58
  decorative, 54, 92
Post attachments, 19
Posts
  building up, 75
  erecting, 77–78
  heights and loads, 24–27
Prefabricated decking, 21
Preservatives, 21, 84–86
Professionals, how to choose, 13–14

Railings, hand, 31, 35, 43, 46, 49, 53, 60, 62–63, 80
Railing supports, securing, 28, 80

Rail-to-post connections, 28
Rain, 8
Ramps, 31, 80
Rise, in steps, 30
Roof decks, 5, 11, 43, 60–61

Salts, as preservative, 85–86
Salvaged materials, 68
Sapwood, 20
Scale drawing 9–11, 23
Screens, 28–29, 36, 37, 43, 44, 45, 46, 48, 58, 61
Screen supports, securing, 28, 80
Screws, 76, 93–94
Sealers, 87
Setback & side yard limitations, 6
Shake, as defect, 20
Site, preparing the, 70–71
Sites, difficult, 11–12
Snow loads, 8
Softwood, 20, 25, 26, 95
Soils engineers, 13
Spacing deck lumber, 23–24, 80–81
Spans & spacings, specifications for, 24–27
Splash lines, 87
Splicing, 74–75
Split-level decks, 40–41
Square-edge lumber, 16
Squaring corners, 73
Stains, deck, 86
Steel, 18, 50, 51
Steps and stairs, 30–31, 64–65, 80
Storage, 63, 82
Streetside decks, 36–37
Stringers, 30
Structural engineers, 13
Subcontractors, 13
Subflooring, 16, 24
Substructure, 15, 17–18, 24–27, 51, 67, 74–79
Sun, seasonal influence of, 7
Surface
  materials, 15–17
  patterns, 23–24
Surfaced lumber, 20, 94

Tile, as deck surface, 16–17
Timber, 17, 20
Tongue-and-groove lumber, 16, 24, 67, 81
Traffic patterns, 10
Tread-to-riser ratios, 30

Variances, 6
Varnishes, 87
Vertical grain, 20

Wane, 20
Warping, 84
Water, decking around, 49, 52–53, 57, 58
Waterfalls, recirculating, 54, 58, 92
Waterfront decks, 38, 39, 52–53, 56
Waterproof finishes, 87
Weeds, controlling, 71
Western Wood Products Association, 21
Wind, 8
Wiring, electrical, 88–89
Wood, for decking, 16, 17, 19, 20–21, 23–28, 67–69, 94, 95

Zoning laws, 5, 6

## Photographers

**Robert Cox:** 39 bottom, 41, 54 top, 64 bottom. **Barbara Gibson:** 46 top. **Steve W. Marley:** 33, 35 top, 36, 38 top, 42, 43, 44, 45, 46 bottom, 47, 48, 52, 53 top right, 53 bottom, 55, 56 bottom, 58, 59 top, 60, 62 top, 63 top right, 63 bottom right. **Ells Marugg:** 38 bottom, 39 top, 49, 63 top left. **Jack McDowell:** 34, 35 bottom, 37, 40, 50, 51, 53 top left, 56 top, 57, 59 bottom, 61, 62 bottom, 63 top center, 63 bottom left, 64 top. **Norman A. Plate:** 54 bottom.